Managing International Business

SELF-DEVELOPMENT FOR MANAGERS
A major series of workbooks for managers edited by Jane Cranwell-Ward.

This series presents a selection of books in workbook format, on a range of key management issues and skills. The books are designed to provide practising managers with the basis for self-development across a wide range of industries and occupations.

Each book relates to other books in the series to provide a coherent new approach to self-development for managers. Closely based on the latest management training initiatives, the books are designed to complement management development programmes, in-house company training, and the management qualification programmes such as CMS, DMS, MBA and professional qualification programmes.

Other books in the series:

Thriving on Stress
Jane Cranwell-Ward

Accounting for Managers
Roger Oldcorn

Managing Change
Colin Carnall

Developing Assertiveness
Anni Townend

Effective Problem Solving
Dave Francis

The Self-reliant Manager
Chris Bones

Step-by-step Competetive Strategy
Dave Francis

Effective Marketing
Geoffrey Randall

Improving Environmental Performance
Suzanne Pollack

Developing the Manager as a Helper
John Hayes

The New Flexi-manager
David Birchall

Making Sense of the Economy
Roger Martin-Fagg

Negotiating a Better Deal
P. Fleming

Jane Cranwell-Ward is at Henley Management College. She is the author of *Managing Stress* (Pan, 1986).

Managing International Business

Neil Coade

INTERNATIONAL THOMSON BUSINESS PRESS
I T P An International Thomson Publishing Company

London • Bonn • Boston • Johannesburg • Madrid • Melbourne • Mexico City • New York • Paris
Singapore • Tokyo • Toronto • Albany, NY • Belmont, CA • Cincinnati, OH • Detroit, MI

To my inspiration, Sandra and Peanut.

Managing International Business

Copyright © 1997 Neil Coade

First published by International Thomson Business Press

I(T)P A division of International Thomson Publishing Inc.
The ITP logo is a trademark under licence

British Library Cataloguing-in-Publication Data
A catalogue record for this book is available from the British Library

First edition 1997

Typeset by J&L Composition Ltd, Filey, North Yorkshire
Printed in the UK by Clays Ltd, St Ives plc, Suffolk

ISBN 0-41513-919-8

International Thomson Business Press
Berkshire House
168–173 High Holborn
London WC1V 7AA
UK

International Thomson Business Press
20 Park Plaza
13th Floor
Boston MA 02116
USA

http://www.itbp.com

— *Contents*

— *List of figures*

— *Series editor's preface*

Managers are facing a growing need to be able to operate in an international arena. Some of these managers may be employed by an international organization and are required to go and work overseas; others may become involved with helping their organizations extend their business internationally. Often these organizations have operated exclusively to serve a home market. Still others may be interested in extending their knowledge and understanding of international business strategy.

Managing International Business has been written with several groups of reader in mind. It has been written primarily for managers required to operate in overseas markets. These managers need to develop international strategic capability very quickly to survive. Managers undertaking courses of study will also find this book readable and helpful.

The book follows a six-stage process in a practical way supported by a range of business case examples. It follows a workbook format, with exercises to be undertaken by the reader to develop understanding in applying the concept to her/his situation.

Neil Coade was chosen to write this book for his extensive background and experience of international business. He works as a consultant advising companies and lectures on MBA programmes on international issues. Previously he completed an MBA himself, at Henley Management College.

Managing International Business is included in the Self-development for Managers Series. This series has been devised to help practising managers develop themselves in the key competencies, which span strategic functional and personal capabilities.

Jane Cranwell-Ward
Series Editor

— *Preface*

Definitions of international business do not really do justice to the one key to success which is the effective management of the whole process. This book will explore some of the ups and downs of this adventure and focus on understanding the business environment, analysing the target market, deciding on the market entry strategy, developing a sustainable competitive advantage, people management and the future global issues facing international companies. A broad definition of international business could be business activities which are conducted across international borders, but as borders cease to exist in the formal sense of the past we are faced with the need for a new definition of international business that encompasses the changes taking place in the modern business environment.

My definition would focus on the complex nature of international activities, the interrelatedness of the whole process and the need to understand a variety of emerging and established business cultures.

You need to be strongly encouraged to develop a view on your own organization and you could begin this by clarifying your thinking on the following issues:

- Are your products/services easily adaptable to international markets?
- Is your organization structured to take advantage of international opportunites?
- Does your company have internationally recognized procedures throughout the company?
- How recognizable is your company brand on the international stage?
- Do customers view the company as an international entity?

I have found in several years of teaching and consultancy in the area of international business that there are few books that focus on the management aspects of assessing, breaking into and operating in international markets. This book is aimed at you, the international manager looking for help in developing your business operations on an international scale.

Let me tell you about this book and why it has been written. In discussing international issues with potential and practising international managers it occurred to me that no one was listening to their specific market needs. There are books that deal with understanding the changing business environment, competitive advantage and international management, but nothing that acts as a survival guide for managers in often new and highly volatile business situations. My opening premise is to treat the reader as someone who has been parachuted into unknown territory and is learning how to survive and prosper in a hostile environment. I have attempted to unveil some of the mysteries surrounding international business and to provide the reader who may be new to the whole concept of international business with a guide through the maze of decisions to be taken and options to be considered. This book will enable you to:

- understand the key elements of market analysis required to launch a new business successfully in an overseas market;
- influence the formulation of international business strategy in a company;
- effectively construct a dynamic market entry strategy for your business;
- design an organizational and management strategy which could respond to the changing needs of the customer and the market environment;
- enable managers to search for a competitive advantage in an increasingly complex and competitive environment.

I will remove some of the stress involved in considering the tasks that accompany international business management. This book is a practical book and it contains exercises that will assist your thinking and help your decision-making processes. There is the element of the workbook about this text which I hope you will not find too cumbersome or authoritarian.

The concept of international business is often considered too complex and risky for some sectors of industry and commerce even to consider. This was driven home to me, early in my career, when I was asked to discuss market entry strategies with a group of furniture manufacturers based in London. Even when the opportunity was spelt out to these companies – here was a golden opportunity to enter the Scandinavian markets and there was government assistance available for interested companies – they were still very reluctant even to consider placing their products into new markets. Therefore the underlying philosophy of this book is to help you understand the pressures and opportunities that exist in the international arena and, above all, to boost your confidence and keep the whole process as simple as possible.

This book has been written for three types of people:

1 Potential or existing international managers who are dropped into unknown territory.
2 Management and business students who possess aspirations to one day suffer the ordeals of the above.
3 Teachers and consultants who assist managers in acting as sounding boards for some of the more difficult questions facing international managers.

The term 'business' is an all-encompassing term which could be applied to the retail sector as well as to manufacturing or financial services. In addition, the term 'product' is used as a generic term and it includes service-based organizations. I have deliberately included examples of companies who do not directly market a particular product but generate income from a whole series of services which may actually be offered to the market in the form of products, for example management consultancy services.

Teachers of management may find the structure of this book quite inviting as an aid to practical exercises that may be conducted as part of a classroom activity or a distance-learning programme. My experience has taught me that managers tend to learn from trying out concepts and exercises in a relatively non-threatening environment; this book could be used in that learning process. Managers may feel comfortable using their own company or an organization that they have recently researched or discussed in group work as an example to experiment with.

The six-stage approach means that you can take an individual stage with a class of international business managers or management students and examine it in some detail. For example, Chapter 3 could be used as part of a management development programme where managers are provided with a market entry scenario and requested to collect market information to underpin their presentations on the best or most workable market entry strategy. This is only one example and I will discuss this example in more detail in the main body of the book. The stages of the book will be integrated to ensure a feeling of continuity for the reader.

The key argument of this book will be based on the view that success in international business is built on effective management and that underpinning this approach is a long-term view of international business strategy and its implementation.

I wish to thank Jane Cranwell-Ward, the series editor, who provided me with the opportunity to write this book, and I also wish to thank Francesca Weaver and Caroline Laws at International Thomson Business Press/Routledge for publishing the book and for their continued support throughout the project.

I would also like to extend my thanks to the individuals from a collection of companies who have allowed me to discuss international business issues with them, including Inter-Continental Hotels, British Telecommunications, the English Tourist Board, British Gas, BP Oil, Mercury Communications and Unilever.

The love and support of my wife Sandra and Peanut have been a source of energy for me throughout the writing of this book.

I would like to open this book and complete this introduction by using a quote from a leading strategic planner in one of the UK's top companies: 'You have to make at least forty-four mistakes before you get it right in international business; this is often the only way to learn.' That means the odds are 44:1, so good luck in your search for international success.[1]

Neil Coade
London, 1996

— *Introduction*

HOW TO USE THIS BOOK

This book acts as a survival guide for the international manager and takes a practical approach to the key issues. It is structured around six stages and the main objective is to assist you in answering the issues that face your international business. These issues may focus on the following aspects of international business:

- Do you understand the international business environment?
- Have you explored all the possibilities in terms of market entry strategies for your business?
- How sustainable is your competitive strategy?
- Do you have the correct people and organization in place to exploit the international business opportunity fully?
- How did you research the market and analyse business opportunities?
- Are you aware of the global issues likely to affect your business in the next five years?

These questions and others will be at the front of your mind when you are reading this book. The techniques I have outlined will assist in answering these questions. The book is written from the perspective of international managers entering new markets or reassessing their company's presence in established markets. Success requires that a number of factors exist before an international business strategy can be deemed to be workable. These factors are highlighted in Figure I.1.

There are many books on international business which have a strong emphasis on marketing strategy but not on the basic considerations of a manager when entering an international market. This book fills that gap. The structure and themes of the book are

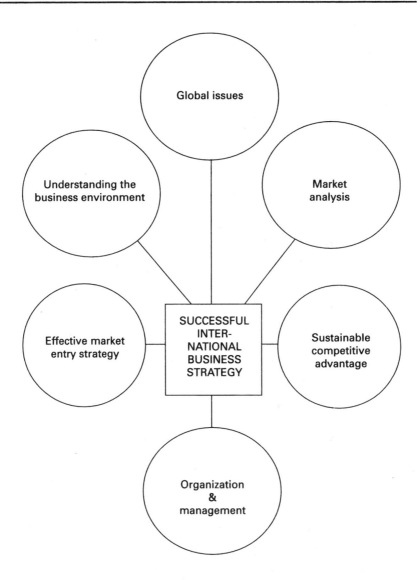

Figure I.1 The key factors for success in international business

CHAPTERS	LEVELS OF UNDERSTANDING/ READER SKILLS
1 UNDERSTANDING THE BUSINESS ENVIRONMENT:	Reader awareness and knowledge of international business
2 MARKET ANALYSIS:	Information sources and identification of market opportunities
3 DEFINING THE MARKET ENTRY STRATEGY:	Design and development of market entry strategies
4 DEVELOPING A SUSTAINABLE COMPETITIVE ADVANTAGE:	Managing the competitive pressures within an international company
5 ORGANIZATION AND MANAGEMENT:	Effective people management in flexible international structures and systems
6 GLOBAL ISSUES FOR COMPANIES:	Analysis and understanding of the competing factors affecting the international business of the future

Figure I.2 Structure and themes of the book

illustrated in Figure I.2 and will provide the reader with an easily accessible and constructive method of assessing the skills needed to enter new markets successfully. The approach to a market will be examined, thus enabling a company to develop a successful market position and maintain a sustainable competitive advantage. During the market entry phase the manager needs to deploy a variety of skills and techniques, including:

- analysis and understanding of the new market;
- strategy formulation and implementation;
- clear knowledge of the key competencies of the existing business.

These skills and techniques and many others will be fully explored within this text.

This book will be based on what has worked in practice and will draw extensively on my experience and research with companies who are actively involved in international business. Many of the ideas have already been developed through my teaching on management development programmes in international business and my research interests in international companies.[1]

CREATING THE FOUNDATIONS OF SUCCESS THROUGH STRATEGY

The foundations of success for any international company have to be built on a well thought out and implemented corporate strategy. Strategy is often very difficult to articulate and it may involve turning the business on its head or at least re-evaluating its competitive position. My perspective is based on the view that strategy is a practical area of management and it concerns the development of a strategic direction for a business. It is focused on the future and it aims to bring about a synthesis of company activities which will achieve the overall objectives set by senior management.

The foundations of success will be built on a clear understanding and existence of the following:

- strategic management;
- senior management commitment;
- clear company vision and values;
- building corporate values;
- establishing an international corporate culture;
- localization vs globalization.

Strategic management

Strategic management is a term used by managers in a variety of international organizations and will be concerned with the long-term direction and scope of an organization. It is also crucially concerned with how that organization positions itself in relation to the international business environment, and in particular to its competitors. It is concerned with establishing competitive advantage, ideally sustainable over a period of time by taking a long-term perspective. You may use the term 'strategy' a great deal in your own company but you may find it quite difficult to manage its implementation.

Strategic management is focused on future orientation, understanding the future and its effects on your company and making strategic decisions; developing an integrated approach to the implementation of international business strategy and the formalization of your thinking on company systems and procedures.

Senior management commitment

This is a crucial factor in ensuring the success of your international business strategy because it underpins the strategic intent of the company in terms of international expansion. The ultimate commitment of the board of directors is the key to ensuring that the international business strategy is effective. Commitment to individual projects may be managed by the strategic planning function of the company through the provision of the three key elements of company commitment, namely:

- senior management time;
- financial resource allocation to specific projects;
- the appointment of key people to new projects.

Clear company vision and values

What are company values and vision?

A vision is a statement that can be understood by everyone in the international company; it is about setting the agenda, making an enduring strategic intent, revising old established company approaches and assisting managers to understand the implementation issues concerned with strategy. 3M, the US manufacturing giant, operates across the globe, with 50 per cent of its sales being made outside the US, and is one of the most innovative companies in the world. The company produces and develops thousands of new products every year and has quietly kept up its solid growth, without the fuss, managerial upheaval or vast write-offs common within some large US multinational companies.

The corporate culture of 3M has developed over the last hundred years of its existence. The company has a very clear understanding of the techniques and systems that are required to make the international operations function effectively. The company has established a serious focus on the customer and the key to its success, namely innovation.[2] The corporate values of the business serve to motivate and support managers throughout the globe and they are the following:

- satisfying customers with superior quality and value;
- providing investors with an attractive return through sustained, high-quality growth;
- being a company that employees are proud to be a part of;
- respecting their social and physical environment.

Exercise 1: Implementing vision statements

Consider the vision statement developed by 3M and its likely impact on the international management of the organization:

- to be the most innovative enterprise
- to be the preferred supplier

Spend thirty minutes examining the likely impact of the 3M vision on the way individual subsidiaries may interpret this vision and consequently operate throughout the globe:

- How is it likely to affect decision-making throughout the company?

- Will the strategy of company subsidiaries be influenced by the vision?

- What impact is it going to make on the search for new products?

- Can this vision motivate employees within an international business?

- Other Comments:

Exercise review:

The vision statement is assisting managers throughout the world to focus on improving the internal effectiveness of operations and to enhance the entrepreneurial activities and capabilities of the business. The wording of the vision statement is quite specific and the enhancement of entrepreneurial activity within the company is a major corporate objective of the senior management team. The view of the company is that the need for enterprise has to be clearly stated if employees are to take a lead from the senior managers within the company. This vision is supported by a series of activities, systems and incentives to reinforce the need for continuous innovation.

You may want to consider two aspects of the 3M vision statement:

■ the practical implementation of the vision statement

■ the leadership potential of the value system of an international company

Building corporate values

International businesses recognize that defining and implementing the right corporate values is a top priority for them and a vital influence on the success of their organization. Real corporate values are based on what people really believe, as in the case of Digital, Levi Strauss and IBM. The process of strategy implementation is very difficult to manage, particularly when you have to consider the impact your decisions may have on the interests of the various stakeholders and the ways in which they may affect the corporate values. The stakeholders include shareholders, government, trade unions, customers, employees and suppliers, and they all need to be convinced that the international strategy being proposed by your company will safeguard their interests and reinforce the long-term values of the business.

The corporate values which help to serve all stakeholders,

including customers, employees and shareholders, and which make sense in a company's new world are the foundations for effective visions and strategies. These shared values can transform the performance of people within a company. Clear and common values provide guidelines for behaviour, a secure framework in which international expansion can take place. The conversion of general values into operational practice requires that managers and supervisors are clear about the values and feel confident in communicating them throughout the company.

The stakeholders will include the following:

- government;
- shareholders;
- trade unions;
- customers;
- employees;
- suppliers.

Exercise 2: Managing stakeholder concerns

The stakeholders of an international company will expect to be consulted in detail about the planned strategy of any management team and it is unrealistic to expect total agreement from all the parties involved. The interests and concerns of each set of stakeholders will differ when a company is considering international expansion. Outline under each of the headings below the likely concerns of each group if your company or a company of your choice was considering international development in the near future.

- Government

- Shareholders

■ Trade unions

■ Customers

■ Employees

■ Suppliers

Exercise review:

My thoughts on this exercise are that you may find it difficult to reconcile the interests of all the stakeholders and managing the impact on the corporate values could prove quite difficult. It may be useful to consider the experience of the Nissan Car Company outlined at the close of this section (see pp. xxiii–xxv).

■ Comments

Establishing an international corporate culture

The corporate culture of a company will change when its focus becomes more international; even when the organization is transplanting management practices or entering new markets, the corporate culture of the company will be altered. This is because to prosper in international markets a company has to adapt to its operational environment and as it does so the very character of the company will change.

If we examine a series of definitions of corporate culture we can see a different emphasis being placed on the term and its meaning in international companies.

Deal and Kennedy (1982) have described the corporate culture of an organization as 'the way we do things around here'. So it is something intangible, but you will recognize it if you spend enough time in a particular company. It has been viewed by Peters and Waterman (1982) as a set of values or a dominant and coherent set of values conveyed by such symbolic means as stories, myths, legends, slogans, anecdotes and fairy tales.

A third view of corporate culture is outlined by Schein (1985), who states that it is the pattern of basic assumptions that a given group has invented, discovered or developed in learning to cope with its problems of external adaptation and internal integration.

The third definition of corporate culture is the most appropriate in my view for international businesses, in that managing international business is a process of coping with the new business environment that you find yourself operating in and adapting your organization to match that external environment.

Case outline: Motorola

Consider the value systems of the international company Motorola.

Its goal is to be the finest corporation in the world. Every one of the close to 100,000 workers carries a small laminated card setting out the corporate philosophy. The company spends millions of dollars each year on training to ensure that the philosophy is made a reality. The senior management team recognizes that defining and implementing the right corporate values is a top priority for them and vital to the success of their organization.

The Motorola philosophy has three key points:

1 Key beliefs (how we will always act):
   ■ constant respect for people;
   ■ uncompromising integrity.

2 Key goals (what we must accomplish):
   ■ best in class;

- increased global market share;
- superior financial results.

3 Key initiatives (how we will do it):
- six sigma quality;
- total cycle-time reduction;
- product manufacturing and environmental leadership;
- profit improvement;
- empowerment for all in a participative, cooperative and creative workplace.

Motorola has the belief that its corporate values serve all stakeholders in the company and are the foundations of effective visions and international business strategy. The company thinks that its values have a direct impact on people and management actions, customers, quality targets, competitiveness, productivity, innovation and profitability. The company aims to integrate its value system with the operations of the business to enhance performance.

Localization vs globalization

The phrase 'think global, act local' is being used a great deal by international companies and the need to be aware of the local needs of customers is a fundamental prerequisite for success in international markets. Awareness of local needs is affecting many sectors of the economy, including car manufacture, retailing, computer software and restaurants. For example, consider the following:

- McDonalds Restaurants are experimenting with the launch of a vegetarian option for the menu in their North of England outlets, which goes against the tradition of being a hamburger restaurant chain in the UK;
- Toyota has introduced the concept of mass customization into the production of its standard vehicles, which is in direct contrast to the idea of mass production traditionally found in car production;
- IBM has restructured the organization to allow the needs of local customers to be considered when designing computer software programs, which seems to be in contrast to its role as a global solution provider;
- Marks & Spencer are launching franchise programmes in new markets to allow for international expansion on a faster scale

and possibly challenging the traditional methods of managing the company.

Case outline: Nissan Car Company

Many of the issues highlighted in this section are explored very well in the case of the Nissan Car Company. If you examine this case you will see that the company clearly recognized the importance of an international approach to strategic planning and the need for total senior management commitment to that strategic plan. As you read the outline of the case you will observe the need for total senior management commitment to the international strategy of the company. The need for a clear company vision is shown by the use of company principles and the building of corporate values and stakeholder support. The corporate culture of the company has needed to adapt and change and this is emphasized by the use of local suppliers and the setting up of a European Technology Centre in the UK.[3]

In the early 1980s the company was steadily working towards the internationalization of car production. This move was greeted with a mixed response from the general public in Japan and the employees of the company. In 1983 the top union representatives held a press conference to announce their wholehearted opposition to the announcement that production was to be based in other parts of the world. Their opposition at the time centred on the production plant that was being considered for construction in the UK, to take advantage of the emerging European markets.

Following extensive media coverage of the employee relations problems of the company the internal pressure on the senior management of the company was immense. The view on the shop floor was that the company had a strategy which sounded more likely and feasible than the alternative presented by the trade union leaders. The company appointed a new Chief Executive, who had two key objectives: to promote Nissan's international operations and to normalize management and trade union relations.

This change in corporate culture took place, and key managers were asked to change the traditional currents of the business and create a new corporate culture and to turn the attention of the company towards the outside world. The corporate culture was turned around but performance continued to slide and this was evidenced by the following pressures being placed on senior management within the company:

- appreciation of the currency;
- price rises in international markets;
- first operating loss of 20 billion yen for the first half of 1986;
- Nissan was the only firm among Japan's eleven automobile manufacturers to show a loss.

The new corporate philosophy was built around the following statement: 'Our first commitment is to customer satisfaction.'

The emerging Corporate Principles had a clear commitment to international business and building new corporate values. They were:

- to create attractive products by capitalizing on the company's innovative and highly reliable technologies, staying in constant touch with the needs of the global market;
- to focus on global trends, making the world the stage for our activities, and to nurture a strong company that will grow with the times;
- meeting customer needs;
- people development.

This strategic commitment was supported by a strong emphasis on a high percentage of locally manufactured components and a managerial commitment to the target market through the following initiatives:

- placing design and research and development in the target market;
- recruiting a local Chief Executive Officer;
- establishing the Nissan European Technology Centre in the UK;
- aiming to be a Good Corporate Citizen.

The company is adopting a strategy of globalization and this is underpinned by a committed senior management team. The company aims to manufacture two out of three vehicles outside Japan by the end of the century. This is to be managed through a network of three regions including North America, Europe and Asia, and would be implemented through a series of working partnerships, joint ventures and a global manufacturing strategy.

These strategic moves by the company are being made against the background of a growing world automotive industry and increasing production levels, as well as the following:

- increasing urbanization;
- increase in fuel use;
- increase in traffic management and urban planning;
- increase in life expectancy;
- increase in world vehicle fleet;
- increase in annual motor car production.

The demand clearly exists for the product and the supporting services of the industry, and this must contribute to the confidence of senior management in implementing an international business strategy.

Nissan have been affected by all of the issues highlighted: strategic management, senior management commitment, clear company vision and values, building corporate values, establishing an international corporate culture, and localization vs globalization.

Exercise 3: The international challenge for Samsung

Samsung is Korea's largest corporation and has transformed itself from a small trading house to an industrial conglomerate, joining the ranks of the Fortune 500 companies. The total sales of the company are in the billions of dollars and its profitability is in the hundreds of millions. The group consists of thirty companies in various lines of business. The core areas of business are focused on machinery, electronics and chemicals. The way forward for the company is to develop indigenous technologies because it lacks the cutting-edge technology necessary to compete against its major foreign competitors. Samsung is the largest producer of high-technology memory chips but still depends on American equipment, thus limiting its technological advancements. The company has also relied on a low-wage strategy to produce its product range and this has been supported by a centrally planned management structure which has promoted bureaucracy. The company recognized that it needed to change to continue to take advantage of its pre-eminent position in world markets.

Conduct a short research project on Samsung to discover the approach the company adopted to prepare the organization for the year 2000. Consider the following:

- the impact of the new corporate culture;
- increase in the quality of production;
- change in company leadership;
- the contrasting management styles of Koreans and Americans.

The changes are still taking place at Samsung and so far they seem to be accepted by all the stakeholders involved and, most importantly, the employees of the company. The company has attempted to create a company culture that is more focused on international markets and quality of production. The examples that many writers have centred on concern the impact of international strategy on the workings of American companies; I have provided examples of Japanese and Korean companies to contrast with the American companies in this chapter.

THE STAGES IN INTERNATIONAL BUSINESS

Creativity and new thinking are required to ensure success in international business, and there are many examples of companies who have looked at markets in different ways and through the exercise of foresight have gained a competitive advantage. The example of the car manufacturer Daewoo is a good one because it has been creative in a market that is very competitive, if not saturated.

Another classic example is Benetton, which over the last thirty years has created a network-style organization which has found and dominated a niche market across the globe. The Benetton brothers have achieved this success without any formal management education.

The final example is Scandinavian Airline Systems, who in the 1980s adopted a creative international business strategy emphasizing the SAS Euroclass, a new version of business class. The company concentrated the company's products on the niche market of the business traveller and reorganized to provide a service to the specialized customer. SAS was using creativity in products and services to change the corporate culture and develop a creative international business strategy.

Understanding international business is never easy and many businesses have lost a great deal of money in poorly implemented or unstructured sorties into new international markets. The successful companies have spent a great deal of management time in developing an understanding of the international business environment and what international business means to them before they enter a new market. There is no 'quick-fix' answer to success; businesses have to work at becoming more effective and struggle to understand the complexities of the international business environment.

The remainder of this book contains the six stages that enable you to develop a successful approach to managing international business.

1 Understanding the business environment

Understanding the dynamics of the international business environment is a complex process because there are so many factors that can impinge on the success or otherwise of an international business. The business environment is constantly changing and its volatility is increased by the threat of competition and changing business cultures. Strategy requires an understanding of the business motives of individual governments and investors. Strategy is focused on the future and aims to achieve an understanding of the business environment on both a broad level and a more specific level. The broad factors may include the political, economic, social, technological and legal aspects, and may be strongly influenced by the government policy of the target market. The specific factors may include the discovery of the correct match between the company and the business environment and will include an analysis of information on pricing, product range, distribution, methods of promotion, research and development and operations.

This chapter will consider six key areas that have a direct impact on a company's understanding of the business environment:

1 Success and failure in understanding the business environment.
2 The changing nature of the international business environment.
3 The competitive factors influencing the business environment.
4 Need for general environmental scanning.
5 Systemizing the search for international business opportunities.
6 Key factors driving the competitive environment.

SUCCESS AND FAILURE IN UNDERSTANDING THE BUSINESS ENVIRONMENT

Let's consider some examples of companies that have studied the business environment and failed and some that despite the odds seem to have succeeded.

The Virgin collection of companies have to be a success story simply because of the way that they study the business environment and take advantage of the leadership already developed in those markets by the key players. There are three product and service examples that have been successful:

1 Airlines: the company is operating in an established market and can be said to be following a very similar approach to the Laker company of the 1970s. The Airline is focusing on specific segments of the market through its detailed understanding of the business environment and its use of modern marketing techniques to promote, price and publicize the range of products and services offered by the company.

2 Financial services: the company has studied the business environment and followed the ground-breaking work of Direct Line Insurance in building a range of products and services that have a unique appeal to a specific segment of the marketplace. The aim of the company would seem to be to expand the segment of the market to its own advantage. It is following the trend towards a higher understanding of financial services amongst the population and segmenting a market that seems to be growing at a remarkable rate.

3 Confectionery: the soft drinks market in the UK has been fragmenting consistently during the 1990s, with a series of new and interesting combinations being offered by the key producers. Virgin has attacked this market on two levels, competing directly with the major multinationals and competing against the specialist drinks manufacturers. These markets have traditionally been very difficult to enter and the company has shown that by setting very high production targets and competing on price these markets can be penetrated.

Another example of a company which studied the market and took advantage of a market opportunity is Dell Computers. It was amongst the companies who clearly identified a market for personal computers emerging in the 1980s and sidestepped the large multinational companies such as IBM by offering the product but also recognizing that customer service was just as important in terms of the customer as the actual product received by the manufacturer. What did they offer that was different? The following:

- strong emphasis on customer service;
- technological support available to all levels of customer;
- userfriendly machines that directly meet the needs of customers;
- market understanding which enabled a high level of understanding of the changes that where taking place in the business environment.

They managed to take a lead in a market that was so clearly dominated by a few key players in the industry.

The final success story in this group of examples is that of the French bottled water companies, typified by Perrier and Evian, who clearly recognized the broad and specific factors affecting the buying decisions of customers, particularly in the UK market. They recognized that the legal argument in the UK was becoming quite ferocious in its condemnation of the level of purity of tap water in the UK. New legislation was being introduced which confirmed the trend towards health issues. The nature of the industry was changing, with an emphasis on different methods of distribution and segmentation of the marketplace. Customer tastes in food and eating out were also changing quite dramatically. In addition there had been liberalization and deregulation of markets, as well as supermarket proliferation and expansion of shelf space. This has resulted in a change in buying behaviour, with bottled water now costing more per litre than petrol.

Disneyland Paris was a bright light in the strategic plans of the Disney Corporation. Why did the company have such difficulties in trying to transfer a perfectly good business concept into a friendly and well-researched business environment? Many explanations have been put forward, which include the following:

1 Location: the choice of location for the project has been heavily criticized as being too near the competition.
2 Incorrect pricing strategy: pricing was confusing to the end-user of the facility and this sent mixed messages to a very price-sensitive marketplace.
3 Ineffective employee relations: employee relations were not given enough priority in the planning stages of the project.

4 Poor climate: the climate was not favourable and other locations such as Spain would have offered an excellent alternative.

5 American overconfidence: expectations were too high that the business concept would travel very easily to the European market.

6 Product offering was wrong: it needed to be adapted to meet the specific needs of the European customer.

7 Marketing: The initial confusion over price and the poor public relations strategy of the company created a situation that was impossible to manage.

8 The concept is non-transferable: an American business idea of this type has to be based in the United States if it is to have any validity in the mind of the customer.

Exercise 4: Transferring a business concept

An interesting exercise could be conducted in small groups of five or six people. Each member of the group is provided with an outline of an international company's situation within a market. Prior to the group meeting to discuss the key issues of the case, the group is requested to highlight the key challenges facing the company in attempting to transfer a business concept. Each member of the group could be given a simple pro forma, as outlined below, and asked to comment on the following questions, using the space provided to note their responses to key areas:

1 Did the company research the market?

2 What are the managerial difficulties involved in transferring a business concept?

3 Do you believe the concept can be test marketed?

---

4 Could analysis of the business environment help in this instance?

You can extend this list of questions to suit the company you are exploring.

The UK retailing company Marks & Spencer has been established since the 1980s in North America. It has been a very difficult market for the management team to understand and to exploit to its full extent. Two major retailing chains were purchased by Marks & Spencer, but even with their retailing and marketing expertise they could not turn them around. The eighty People's Stores were sold in 1992 and D'Allaird's was downsized and restructured. The Marks & Spencer chain was extended nationwide with what is recognized with hindsight to have been reckless haste.

Why did they find difficulties in the North American market? For the following reasons:

- transfer of the Marks & Spencer concept was difficult;
- there was a lack of market testing and supporting market research;
- senior management perceived the business environments of the UK and North America to be very similar;
- business culture had different approaches to distribution strategy;
- the strategic decision-making process was too distant from the market;
- the search for market share was too ambitious;
- there was a lack of market research focused specifically on the marketplace;
- experience in international trade was lacking;
- company strengths had been developed in the home market and did not apply to the international markets.

Marks & Spencer has had mixed success in terms of international business, but for every apparent failure in terms of international business they have experienced success in another market and, best of all, they have learnt from their experiences.

The experience curve is crucial to the success of international businesses and the success of many companies comes from extending their level of experience.

Marks & Spencer opened its first European branch in Paris in 1975. It now has sixteen stores in France, with more openings planned. The company has five stores in Spain, three in Belgium and two in the Netherlands. The three stores in Ireland are now included in the European arm of the company and expansion is being planned in that part of the world. In March 1995 the company announced that it planned to open new stores in Germany and Italy.

The softly softly approach adopted towards European expansion has been supported by a series of careful pilot schemes to test market products and services prior to full entry into the markets. This approach is now preferred to rapid expansion by using acquisitions.

China is the next target for the company and it is planning expansion through franchising and has spent the last eighteen months on an extensive market research programme. Marketing coordination is being managed by a local marketing team who are aware of the importance of being close to the customer. This focused approach is utilizing the experience that the company gained from its time operating in international markets. The company has probably learnt from its experiences; we will have to wait and see.

THE CHANGING NATURE OF THE INTERNATIONAL BUSINESS ENVIRONMENT

Understanding the changing nature of the business environment is the second key step for an international company.

A new international economic order has emerged across the world, with the balance of trade moving towards the Asia Pacific and new markets starting to dominate the thinking of company strategists. Many companies are in a period of major transition and the list is too long to contemplate. The companies affected include household names such as IBM, who have had to adapt to a new business environment which they had difficulty in predicting.

Two of the reasons for this are the threat of increased competition following the deregulation of sectors of the economy and the changing source of the competitive threat, which seems to be increasingly unpredictable. The economic growth policies established by each country are promoting economic growth as a major focus of their manifesto and this places greater pressure on companies to perform. The outcome is that most business environments are becoming sophisticated or are realizing that they need to improve and are introducing policies to ensure success.

Advancements in technology are increasingly being utilized by companies, who now have a greater level of choice, and the cost of technology transfer is decreasing in some markets. Increasingly, the technology that is available to companies is supported by a range of suppliers who are searching for new applications.

The growth and influence of pressure groups throughout the world is having a profound affect on the thinking of many senior managers in international companies. There is a clear recognition that actions taken in one market will have a direct affect on the customer base of another market. International companies are recognizing the sophistication of these pressure groups, and their influence can be seen in the retail, manufacturing, food production and energy sectors of the world economy.

The changing nature of corporate strategies will be explored in more detail in later chapters of this book, but some of the aspects that influence the corporate strategy are outlined here.

Companies are involved in more intra-company trade, sharing company resources, developing partnerships and discovering new ways to enhance cooperation between functions of the company. There has also been an increase in international service companies which have a global reach and innovative management teams that use technology to seek advancement in company performance.

International businesses are increasingly using some form of licensing as part of their corporate strategy, which enables them to cut across segments of the market and enhance manufacturing capability. International businesses have also focused on franchising as a method of gaining strategic acceptance of a business concept and utilizing the strengths of independent business people. An additional advantage is that franchising can be accepted by governments as a legitimate method of market entry. The increased use of strategic alliances has been gradual in the 1990s, with a long-term view being adopted by many companies, accompanied by a focus on government support for company alliances within one country.

Patterns of organization and management have also had an

impact on the business environment of international businesses. The flexibility of people in terms of their roles and responsibilities within companies has increased and there is an emphasis on new methods of manufacturing. The flexibility of research and development and its link to operational aspects of the business have been recognized as important. The focus on integration of technology, processes and networks is having a profound affect on the way senior management views the business environment.

Decentralization and delegation of responsibility are forming the foundations of corporate strategy in many international businesses. The focus on devolved decision-making is influencing the thinking of senior strategists in many companies and this manifests itself in the design of organizational structure being considered by some international businesses.

All of these changes have repercussions for the employee relations strategies developed by companies, with companies being expected to adopt a proactive and participative style towards employee relations. These issues are also being considered alongside the question of ownership and whether or not a share in the business should be offered to employees in the form of a stakeholding in the company. The acceptance and management of change are becoming key drivers in the management of international businesses.

THE COMPETITIVE FACTORS INFLUENCING THE BUSINESS ENVIRONMENT

The third key step for an international company is understanding the competitive factors influencing its business.

The competitive environment has changed quite dramatically in recent years. The political situation has changed; for example, the march towards market-based economies seems irreversible. This has been managed by the Chinese by means of a new economic mechanism which differentiates Chinese practices from those of capitalist societies.[1] The focus is on the state regulating the market and the market guiding new ventures. Resources also play a key role in terms of the movement of capital, skilled labour and effective management.

Demographics also have a role as a competitive factor because markets are becoming fragmented and growing at a previously unknown rate. For example, in February 1995 China marked the birth of its one billion two hundred millionth citizen. The government used the occasion as an opportunity to champion the cause of family planning. There was little mention in the Chinese press that a decade ago planners hoped they would not see 1.2 billion until after the year 2000. The economist intelligence unit forecasts that China's population will be as high as 1.33 billion by the year 2001. As the most populous nation on earth, China will struggle with population control well into the next century.

Economic performance is a competitive factor, and even Vietnam has been successful in battling high levels of inflation, averaging 300 per cent between 1985 and 1988. By introducing economic measures they have managed to stabilize the currency, increase product availability and reduce the inflationary pressures in the economy. The result of these measures has been a drop in inflation to 30 per cent and the creation of a relatively competitive economy.

The use of communications networks has blossomed in many countries. Even China has entered a period of phenomenal growth in telecommunications. During the 1980s the Chinese telecommunications industry was the fastest-growing in the world. In 1994 the Xinhua News Agency reported that annual Chinese telecom investment grew by over 50 per cent in 1993 and close to 0.25 million long-distance lines were added, more than the total for the preceding three years. Donations of decommissioned exchange equipment from Hong Kong since the mid-1980s, with accompanying technical personnel from China to undertake training and installation/maintenance, helped on a basic level. In China, collaborations with western companies at the leading edge of technology in China's own projects have confirmed the commitment of western companies to developing a world-class telecommunications infrastructure throughout the new market.

The use of capital has been influenced by the investment patterns and trends being set by companies over the last decade. The criteria for investment have changed for many companies and the methods of investment promotion have changed. A focus on cooperation and sharing resources has also emerged, as in the production-sharing contracts being set up in Vietnam.

Transportation and logistics are proving to be an advantage for many companies and this sector is attracting a high level of investment from individual governments and companies entering new markets. Companies are investing heavily in logistics as a mainstay of their international competitive strategies. A series of initiatives is being introduced by companies and governments which place a strong emphasis on cross-border cooperation.

The environment can emerge as a key consideration when entering a new business environment, depending on the sensitivity of customers and governments to the effect business actions can have on the wellbeing or otherwise of the business environment. The design and implementation of policies and strategies by companies can help towards gaining a greater level of awareness and understanding of the position taken by a particular company on the key environmental issues.

NEED FOR GENERAL ENVIRONMENTAL SCANNING

Scanning the business environment is an activity that needs to be conducted on a continual basis by all international businesses. The reasons are diverse, but particularly important is the need to be aware of the threat of competition and the attractiveness of specific business opportunities.

The benefit of operating in many economies is that you avoid downturns in demand in the home market. Manage the damaging changes in the economic cycle in your existing portfolio of businesses. Achieve smooth production flows and aim for steady sales throughout the year.

The reasons for scanning the business environment may include the following four factors:

1 The need to avoid saturation of existing markets:
   - further expansion in your present market may be expensive or impossible;
   - it may not be possible to adapt the technology used by your company or to develop it to suit the needs of existing markets;
   - the introduction of foreign management techniques following takeovers or mergers could place pressure on senior management to seek additional business development opportunities.

2 Being responsive to market changes:
   - sifting opportunities to identify areas of future business activity;
   - devising realistic plans for considering new market opportunities;
   - allowing existing customers' expansion to lead your activities.

3 Extending the sources of supply:
- extending procurement into a new supply chain;
- searching for higher quality/reliability amongst your network of suppliers;
- purchasing suppliers to integrate into your business.

4 Extending the sources of capital, labour and technology:
- introducing cost reductions and effectiveness;
- accessing cheaper capital;
- utilizing flexible and cost-effective personnel;
- searching for diverse sources of finance;
- spreading risk;
- enhancing the employee relations climate;
- implementing new technological applications;
- setting up new communications networks.

SYSTEMIZING THE SEARCH FOR INTERNATIONAL BUSINESS OPPORTUNITIES

The fifth key step for an international company is to systemize the search for an international opportunity and this can best be shown in Figure 1.3, which outlines the process of searching for business opportunies in a flow diagram.

KEY FACTORS DRIVING THE COMPETITIVE ENVIRONMENT

The final step for an international business is to understand what are the key factors influencing the competitive environment of their marketplace. The key factors driving the competitive environment include globalization and increased pressure for integration, particularly in manufacturing and research & development, and building a seamless offer to the customer. The demands of local markets have increased due to the level of customer knowledge and awareness.

The transfer of knowledge and skills is sought very determinedly by developing economies. There is increased pressure to be more customer-responsive and to develop global brands with global advertising campaigns to support the global customer base.

Time-based competition is having an affect on shortening the life-cycles of products and the targeting of products and services to specific customer groups.

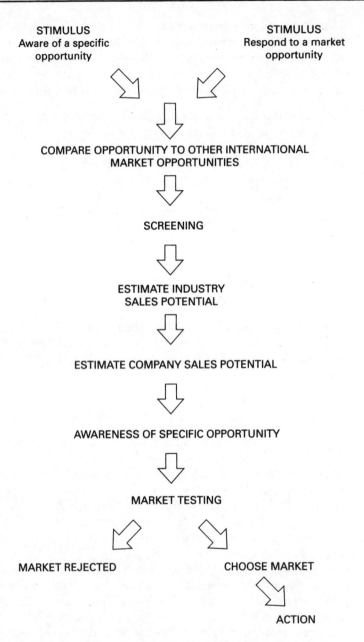

Figure 1.3 Systemizing the search for international business opportunities

Competitive production strategies are being used which place an emphasis on quality improvements being constantly sought by businesses and pre-inspection eradicated in the production of new products. Computerized inventory control systems such as Just in Time are being used to control costs and improve productivity. Supplier networks are being improved, with an increased emphasis on efficiency and cooperation and consistent improvement of supplier performance. Internal and external partnerships are being created across the range of activities of an international business.

The business environment is changing quickly and by following these basic steps the international business of tomorrow can at least have a chance of survival in an increasingly competitive marketplace.

Exercise 5: Relocation for competitive advantage

Global relocation is the method of moving an element of your business outside the home market. It has been stated that companies can achieve a distinct competitive advantage thorough relocating part of their business. Companies can develop a competitive advantage and this is based on improving company processes such as production and research and development. Differentiation may be the goal of an international company attempting to relocate, and this could be focused on improved service, higher quality or advanced technology. This may involve moving the marketing effort of a company closer to the customer or producing the product in a faster, more customer-responsive manner. Often the key driver for relocation is simply cost, and strong influences on cost are distribution, wages and land factors.

Consider the relocation of any part of your business in recent years and the effect it had on operations and the profitability of the company.

■ Comments:

What was the impact on the following aspects of company operations?

◼ communications

◼ technology transfer

◼ risk assessment

◼ independence of the company

2 Market analysis

The power of having a system to gather information from the international marketplace is phenomenal and will help to support any strategic decision being made in the organization. A Japanese approach will be discussed in this chapter and the emphasis of the Japanese on feasibility and test marketing will be examined. The starting point for any international analysis of the market will be the PEST concept, which translates into political, economic, social and technological issues affecting a target market.

An understanding of the PEST concept and its application to the country of your choice has to be supported by an analysis of your company's strengths and weaknesses and how they match the business opportunity you are investigating. Once the match is achieved a process of segmentation will need to take place and this aspect will be explored within this chapter. Exercises will be used to help you consider the key aspects of the design process when introducing an international market information system into your company. One point which is certain is that competent analysis of the target marketplace is fundamental to the success of any international business.

Information is the source of all the key strategic decisions made by international businesses. The availability of information and the security and reliability of the source are important. The source of the information can vary, and the compatibility of the information with existing systems is a necessity. The information needs to comply with the existing information databases you are using in your company, in order to build a greater understanding of the marketplace.

The type of information required to make strategic decisions will depend on the individual company. For example, a senior operations manager in a UK utility company may be looking to an overseas agent to provide the market intelligence that can finally enable the entry decision to be made to go into a particular market. If the go-ahead is not forthcoming the company may decide to shelve the whole project. The same level of urgency may not exist for a product which is entering a fast-moving consumer goods market, where government approval may not have such relevance in the international markets being targeted. Alternatively, a motor car manufacturer may not be as interested in the political aspects of the market but could be very concerned about the economic developments within the target market.

It is very difficult for a company to operate on hearsay or intuition and this is particularly applicable in international markets. The difficulty is achieving the right level of complexity and accessibilty to the information is a challenge for the management team introducing the systems for market analysis.

KEY CONSIDERATIONS IN USING INFORMATION SYSTEMS TO MAKE INTERNATIONAL BUSINESS DECISIONS

The advantage of effective information in making business decisions is not appreciated by every international company but it has a far-reaching effect on the understanding of new international markets. The effective use of information can have the following positive outcomes in managing an international business:

1 Reducing uncertainty in choice of target market. You cannot predict the future but you can achieve a deeper understanding of the complexities of the business environment. The learning process for your company will start to take place when you are operating in your target marketplace. The market information system provides you with a set of bearings to work with when you are considering how to enter a new market.

2 Managing risky new investments. As you learn about the process of information-gathering you will learn a great deal about your weaknesses and strengths as an organization. The process of information-gathering is long, painstaking and difficult. Your company will need to provide a well-researched foundation of data before you will be able to consider the strategic options open to your management team.

3 Achieving a balance between cost and value. The market entry strategy of a company is a difficult and complex task and requires a

wide range of information to be collected before accurate decisions can be considered. Each customer contact, employee, distribution system and stakeholder is a source of information. The role of the information specialist is to collect information from whatever source is appropriate and then to start to generate market entry strategies for the management team to consider. The balance between cost and value has to be achieved and the cost of information-gathering can only be assessed by examining the success of the market entry strategies.

4 Cost-effective acquisition of information. Ascribing a price to information is quite difficult, but you can set a price for undertaking market research or establishing listening posts of various types in the target market. The price of information will be difficult to set but the management and marketing teams within the company must be able to answer three questions at any time:

■ How strong is demand for our products or services?
■ What are our competitors thinking?
■ Is customer reaction to our company positive or negative?

5 Managing the information-collection process. The process of collecting and establishing a market information system is not easy and will require continuous monitoring of information from the competition, market and customer. The immediate desire to enter a new marketplace has to be tempered with an understanding of the nature of the market and how it is likely to develop in the short and long term. There are some examples of companies entering a market unannounced, with very little knowledge of the market and only the perceived opportunity to guide them.

6 Developing an appropriate classification, storage and retrieval system. The classification of information is of crucial importance because it will underpin the use of the system by a range of international managers throughout the company. The market entry strategy will not be developed in isolation; it will form an intrinsic part of the corporate and marketing strategy of the company. Therefore, the classification systems used to search the information have to be understood by the relevant departments or functions concerned with corporate strategy.

7 Ensuring competence in analysis. The analysis of the information is central to the success of your information system. The information system has to be viewed as an important focal point for the strategic planning that takes place in the business. Above all, the

system has to be an integral part of decision-making and should not be seen as something quite complex and non-accessible to managers on a global basis. The key aim of the information system is to make it userfriendly to managers and employees throughout the business.

Let's look at the experience of one international business manager when asked by a UK company engaged in manufacturing high-quality steels for the European and American markets how he would assess potential new markets for their products. The international business manager replied that he would start by undertaking detailed desk research in London, and once he was convinced of the appeal of the potential market he would go and visit the market, taking a great deal of time to understand how the market functioned and discussing the market opportunities with competitor companies and potential customers.

This answer was taken as being a little flippant and over-simplistic by the senior management team who had put the question to the manager. The senior management team were expecting more structure and detail to accompany the answer. It may have been a sketchy answer to the question but in essence this is the approach that has been followed by successful companies in researching and entering international markets (see Figure 2.4).

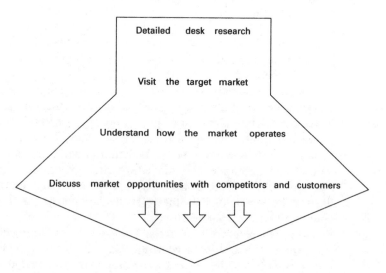

Figure 2.4 Putting the basics in place

CLASSIC MARKET STUDIES BY JAPANESE FIRMS

Market studies have enabled the Japanese to build a great deal of international success over the last twenty-five years. Japan has approached market entry strategy in classic textbook fashion.[1] The Japanese carefully analyse market opportunities through exhaustive market feasibility studies before entering any market. They first search for attractive opportunities that match the economic goals of the Japanese economy. Then, following the key aspects of the marketing concept, they develop products that customers want or need.

Once products are developed, market entry points and timing of entry are chosen, with the objective of obtaining a strong initial share of the market. Once an initial foothold is established, the market entry strategy then shifts to market penetration tactics which broaden the customer base while continuing to expand market share.

Japan's strategy for market entry has followed the classic philosophy of market segmentation and product positioning. Japanese marketing tactics are effectively described by the teachings of Miyamoto Musashi (1645), which emphasize the strategic advantage of knowing the environment throughly, seizing the initiative and forestalling the enemy at every point. No other Musashi strategic prescription describes more accurately the typical Japanese approach to market segmentation and product positioning than his approach entitled 'To injure the corners':

> It is difficult to move strong things by pushing directly, so you should injure the corners. In large scale strategy, it is beneficial to strike at the corners of the enemy's force. If the corners are overthrown, the spirit of the whole body will be overthrown. To defeat the enemy you must follow up the attack when the corners have fallen.
>
> (Musashi 1645: 78)

Japan's entry into the US automobile market was developed along the lines of the 'injure the corners' strategy, with their deep penetration into the compact car market in the 1970s and early 1980s.

Japanese managers continuously seek out the best in engineering, management and marketing techniques throughout the world, often copying in detail how business is being conducted. They gather foreign technical and scientific information, memorize it and, then, more often than not, they improve upon the techniques contained within the original concepts or products.

Supporting the detailed analysis of the market is the pivotal role played by pricing strategy. This is probably the most important variable in market entry strategy, yet a surprising number of companies have neither consistent nor explicit pricing objectives. Pricing is often set entirely on the basis of cost, independently from the rest of the marketing mix and with little regard for overall marketing strategy and objectives.

This can be a critical mistake in marketing strategy, especially in competitive situations with Japanese international businesses. The Japanese continually exploit the fact that American companies base price on profitability objectives rather than share of the market. In positioning a product in a target market, the Japanese apply a market-share pricing strategy which deliberately uses a low entry price to build up market share and establish a long-run dominant market position. The Japanese tend to set the prices of their products much lower than their competitors to attract potential customers, and are content to accept losses in the early stages of market entry to ensure a long-term position of market development in a particular market.

The close link between price and product quality is the critical feature of the Japanese market entry strategy. The Japanese exercise a great deal of patience in entering new markets and they are not concerned with short-term profitability but long-term growth. The aim is for a firm position in the marketplace which will provide rewards over the long term. It is not uncommon for Japanese companies to plan as far ahead as twenty years, with some large corporations planning 150 years ahead.

THE PEST CONCEPT

The analysis provided by the PEST concept will be complemented by a market information system which allows in-depth analysis to take place. Market segmentation techniques can also be used successfully to pinpoint the needs and wants of particular customer groups. This concept is frequently quoted by international managers and academics as the starting point for analysing new markets. The initials stand for:

- Political factors influencing a market;
- Economic situation confronting the new market entrant;

■ Social structure and systems operating within the market;
■ Technology available and developed in the target market.

The key point of the concept is that it gives you a 'snapshot' of the potential marketplace, as shown in Figure 2.5.

Examples of the political issues raised by the PEST concept are as follows:

■ What is the political structure of the target market?
■ How is foreign capital viewed by the government of the new market and are there any restrictions on the movement of capital?
■ What is the role of the private sector of the economy in relation to the public sector? The government may be encouraging private ownership and a commercial ethos within the public sector, which helps to build a dynamic economy.

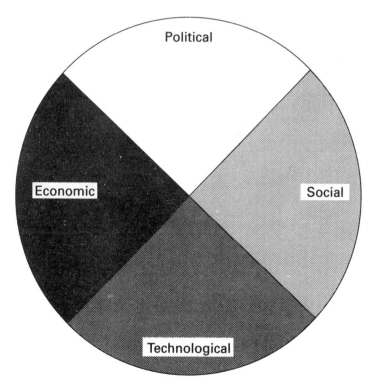

Figure 2.5 The PEST concept

The following are some of the economic issues:

■ At which stage of the business cyclical, pre-growth or recession is the timing right to enter the market?
■ In which direction are economic indicators such as interest rates and inflation heading?
■ Are the levels of disposable income within the economy increasing or decreasing?

Social factors which must be considered are:

■ Is the employee relations culture in the target market conducive to business? What is the level of strikes and stoppages in industry?
■ Is there social mobility and movement of skilled people across the target market?
■ Is educational support available throughout the economy and what are the methods being used? The number and quality of key people is also important; for example, the number of engineering, business, technology and computer-science graduates available in the market.

Technological factors are also important:

■ Does national research and development expenditure compare favourably with the competition?
■ Does technology transfer provide an opportunity to gain a competitive advantage in the marketplace?
■ Is technological expertise available to support service and product development within your business?

Exercise 6: Using PEST analysis

List the factors that you would consider important in a PEST analysis of a target market of your own choice.

Target market:

■ Political factors

■ Economic factors

■ Social factors

■ Technological factors

INFORMATION GAPS

The PEST analysis has to be supported by a detailed piece of analysis which will enable you to start to design a market entry strategy to penetrate the target market successfully. PEST analysis, as I have already stressed, is a starting point for your analysis and does not give you an indication of how the business will function in reality when faced with the pressures of the target market. The question that needs to be answered is how you fill the gaps in information that are required by the business.

The information gaps will include several areas of company activity.

Sales information

The sales forecasts for the target market are a crucial indicator of market potential and these will form the basis of a series of sales targets for the marketing function of the business. The sales structure cannot be designed without having a clear understanding of the sales potential of the market and how this is likely to improve in the future. The structure of the sales effort of the company will provide you with an indication of the sales methods that are most appropriate for the target market.

Market share

The potential market share for your organization is an important piece of information and can only be discovered by detailed analysis of the target market. The competitive analysis will give you an indication of who the key players are in your target market and of the methods that can be used to break up their share of the marketplace. Once you have a share of the market you will require an understanding of how to defend your position against the threat of new competition or substitute products or services.

Demand forecasting

Demand forecasting is probably the most important element of your market analysis because unless a clear level of demand has been identified for your product you will have difficulty in surviving in the marketplace. Continuity of demand is important and any changes in the nature of demand need to be addressed by the marketing team as soon as possible. The influences on demand have to be identified by your company before you enter the new market and these have to be monitored to recognize any changes that could affect the market position of the company.

Operating costs

Understanding the nature of the operational costs involved in running the business in the target market is important because the cash flow of the new venture can be dramatically affected by inaccurate forecasting. It is important to estimate the setting-up costs and this process can often be too subjective if left to the discretion of managers who have a vested interest in the success or failure of the new project. The operational and on-going costs have to be realistic to withstand the rigour of independent and objective analysis. The basic factors of production must be considered at this point, including the cost of capital, land and people.

Level of assets deployed

An estimate must be made of how much capital is needed to start penetration of the target market. The organization will need to calculate how an increase in assets is to be managed, whether it is required and how the increase will be financed. The level of assets to be deployed in a new venture may increase by an amount significant enough to warrant a joint venture or a partnership of vested interests to secure a higher level of investment in the target market.

Profitability levels

The expected profitability levels for the new venture have to be forecast and a comparison can be made between the target-market and industry-sector average rates of profitability of previously entered markets. The pricing strategy chosen by the company has to reflect the profitability forecasts of the marketing and strategic planning functions of the business. Flexibility in profitability targets may be required by the management team as they initially try to secure a foothold in the market and build market share.

International risk factors

Each company will have some idea of the level of risk it is prepared to contemplate in entering a new market. The level of risk may be guided by previous investments or by advice taken from the investors supporting the company strategy. Risk factors may change, but it is quite difficult to manage uncertainty and many companies will be attempting to manage the unexpected when entering new markets. The response of the competition in the target market will have a profound effect on the success of your entry strategy or analysis of the market and, besides the obvious response of a price war, can be very difficult to predict.

Degree of flexibility

The degree of flexibility in responding to the changing needs of specific customer groups can be a fundamental part of your analysis of a market. The response of companies to the feedback they receive from customers, in terms of changing levels of service or altering the product, can play an important role in building competitive advantage. The flexibility that can be added to the operational capability of your company can enable you to respond more quickly to changes in the marketplace. Technological innovations can provide you with an advantage in a new market because the competition may find it difficult to respond to the needs of the marketplace if they have dated operational systems or technology.

Management

The availability of effective management skills is essential if you are to manage the entry into a new market successfully and take advantage of the element of surprise. The standard of management thinking has to be very high and management must develop a creative approach to entering new markets. General management skills are required and these have to encompass an understanding of new venture management, marketing, financial systems and business transformation. This knowledge and these skills have to be reinforced by a comprehensive system of management development across the company.

Exit strategies

The analysis of a new market is a complex task and must be accompanied by a detailed entry strategy. The entry strategy must be supported by an exit strategy which can enable the international business to manage its time in the target market successfully. The company may be asked to rationalize operations or restructure the organization in a cost-cutting exercise and it cannot afford to be hampered by the arrangements it has made whilst entering the market. These arrangements might focus on long-term contracts for the supply of raw materials, exclusive access to a distribution network or the negotiation of government contracts or entry conditions. A long-term approach which has built-in contingency plans for the future of the business must be considered by international businesses.

MARKET ANALYSIS AND SEGMENTATION

Market analysis is central to the international strategy being pursued by a company. It is often expensive and is necessary to enable a company to make sound strategic decisions. The market analysis must be focused on the future.

Let's consider the example of Andersen Consulting, who, in common with their competitors in the 1980s, were busy analysing the changing market for management consultancy services and products for the forthcoming decade. The aspect that the company was monitoring which was not being followed by the competition was the changing nature of the information technology market, which to all intents and purposes was a different market . Andersen surmised that the customer of the information technology company would be changing and consequently its needs would change. Therefore a new market was being created and subsequently Andersen Consulting found themselves dominating the new marketplace.

An analysis of the market needs to achieve the following successes:

- to determine a new view of emerging markets;
- to establish a long-term focus on how to secure the company's presence in those new markets;
- to be creative in questioning current definitions of the target market;
- to identify the key factors of success in the target markets;
- to discover opportunities for expansion and market development.

The key focus needs to be on customers and allowing them to define the market and their constantly changing needs and aspirations.

International market segmentation will take place once the initial analysis of the marketplace has been undertaken and the match between the company and the market has been explored. You can then start to segment the market for particular products and services which you have on offer. Segmentation of markets is as old as the concept of marketing itself. It is based on the principle that if you segment a market you can reduce risk and target your products or services at specific areas of a market.

Strategies can be based on market segmentation. Market segmentation can be easily defined as the division of the market into customer groups with very similar needs and wants and the influence these have on their buying decisions. Within the market segment there are often very different value systems at work and these underpin the buying decisions made by customers. For example, Marks & Spencer have decided to exclude the corporate brand of St Michael from its products because it is confusing many international customers, who do not recognize the name as having any relevance to the company name of Marks & Spencer, and consequently informing their buying decisions.

Spotting opportunities through segmentation is not easy, but with the power of hindsight we can examine the success of the following companies:

- The American service company Federal Express has made technology play a leading role in shaping the business and segmented a slice of the document transfer business.
- The American multinational 3M has dominated segments of the adhesives market by careful market analysis and market research.
- The UK travel company Trailfinders developed a stronghold in the marketplace by supplying a niche market with tailored products.
- The Korean car manufacturer Daewoo has taken a strategic decision to enter the market in the compact car sector in order to gain a competitive position in an already saturated marketplace.

Exercise 7: Market segmentation

Try to think of another four examples of companies that have successfully segmented markets.

- Company 1:
- Company 2:
- Company 3:
- Company 4:

What are the similiarities in approach of these companies? Use this page to map out some of your thoughts:

- Company 1:

- Company 2:

- Company 3:

- Company 4:

Market segmentation is a fundamental step towards developing a market information system. It has four major advantages:

- establishing a marketing strategy that can offer superior value to the customer;
- making management accept that the superior value can be determined only by the customer;
- grouping customers together into sections called markets and then again into market segments (these can form the basis of a competitive marketing strategy);
- introducing a sufficiently flexible approach to meet the ever-changing needs of different customer bases and beating the competition in the process.

KEY COMPONENTS OF THE INTERNATIONAL MARKET INFORMATION SYSTEM

The design of an international market information system requires a detailed understanding of the current philosophy underpinning market segmentation, an understanding of the decision-making processes of your customers and an analysis of how markets may be changing. This can help you spot integration issues and new market opportunities (see Figure 2.6).

The design criteria of the market information system need to provide security of data, the process must be continually improved and you need to keep an edge to data capture within the international business. The key focus of market information has to be on assisting senior management to make more effective international business decisions.

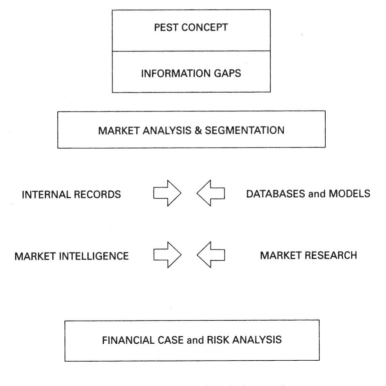

Figure 2.6 An international market information system

The PEST concept is widely used by international managers but it only provides you with a 'snapshot' of the target market and cannot be used on its own. Gaps in information have to be discovered and it is often important to appreciate what you may not know as well as the hard facts about a market. The analysis of a market and the use of market segmentation will assist managers in developing a continuous view of the changing nature of their target markets.

This analysis of the market enables you to understand three key elements of any market and the risk involved in entering a new and unconquered business environment. The three key elements are: market, competition and customers.

3 Defining the market entry strategy

The previous chapter provided you with a broad understanding of the business environment you may be facing as an international business manager and some approaches that could be used to analyse that environment. This chapter enables you to explore the principles of market entry strategy and consider how they may affect your company, identify what market entry strategy you intend to consider and allow you to assess what ideas you need to put into action to change your present approach to market entry. This chapter will include a number of exercises which will assist you in a detailed examination of the challenges facing companies when they enter a market for the first time.[1]

The market entry strategy is crucial to the success of every international business; if you get it wrong it may be difficult to recover your market position. The popularity of each market entry strategy seems to vary from one particular market to another. The popularity of joint ventures is high but there appears to be a strong move towards alliances of one type or another. The popularity of manufacturing is still strong, but because of the high costs involved in establishing a manufacturing facility in a target market the costs may have to be shared by a series of interested parties. Franchising, which grew throughout the 1980s, has remained in the armoury of weapons open to the international business manager.

Whichever choice you decide to make as an international business manager needs to be tempered by an understanding of the effect your choice will have on other elements of the business. The range of problems faced by your company will obviously change from one business to another depending on the size of the business and how ambitiously your company is behaving.

THE PROBLEMS FACED BY THE INTERNATIONAL BUSINESS MANAGER

Poor product positioning

Once you have decided on the market entry strategy you must recognize the effect this is likely to have on the position of your product in the target market. In other words, the market entry strategy will have a direct effect on the perception that the customer has of your product and the offering that you are able to make to the general public. We will explore this issue in more depth in the remainder of this chapter.

Ineffective pricing strategy

The pricing strategy of a company entering a new market is crucial to the success or otherwise of that entry strategy. As we have seen, Japanese companies use the pricing strategy as a very important part of their market entry strategy to undercut the competition and secure their position in the new market. The pricing strategy is the starting point in developing a relationship with a customer: if your pricing is ineffective the customer may not even notice you have entered the marketplace.

Marketing strategy

The marketing strategy of the international business will be dramatically affected by the choice of market entry strategy. The choice of market entry strategy will have a direct effect on how quickly the company can expect to penetrate a specific market, how successfully the company can develop its presence in the market and invest in new product development to reinforce its position. The choice of diversification may be taken away from the company if it approaches the market with an inappropriate market entry strategy, and perhaps the original choice of manufacturing as an entry strategy cannot be adapted to the changing circumstances of the marketplace.

Distribution

An inappropriate market entry strategy can be very problematic for the distribution channels chosen for the product or service that is entering the new market. Distribution of the new product in your chosen market is fundamental to the success of the launch of any new product into a market and the growth of that product. In order to distribute a product in a new market it may be necessary to enter into a distribution agreement with a major player in the target market who can provide access to the effective distribution channels of the target market.

Demotivation

A poor choice of market entry strategy can lead to a rapid demotivation of the production, distribution, marketing and sales departments within the business. The effect on the general management of the company can be traumatic if the wrong choice of market entry strategy has been made. Motivation in many international businesses is important because of the distance often found between the senior management teams who make the decisions and the people who have to implement them.

Strategy confusion

The strategic confusion that can develop when a company has chosen an inappropriate market entry strategy is immense. The internal reputation of specific functions in the company will take a great deal of work to repair. The marketing planners will be considered not really to understand the buying decisions of the customers and will be seen as out of touch. The strategic planners will be seen to be unaware of the changing nature of the business environment and the possible moves made by the competition.

New product development disasters

New product development can often take the form of a new product launch into a new international market. Although the leading managers in some international companies, such as Sony, will state that the company can tolerate mistakes being made, they do not wish these mistakes to be made too often, and prefer that if mistakes are made, people in the company, and particularly managers, learn from these mistakes. An inappropriate market entry strategy may lead to a disaster in the launch of a new product, which can be very difficult to rescue.

Leadership

Strategic leadership, which works in many international companies, is fundamental to their success. The basis of success in international business is having a clear set of corporate values which underpin the activities of everyone in the company. Also helpful is having a vision for the international company that can be very clearly focused on the future and can act as a motivating force for people both inside and outside the company. The choice of an inappropriate market entry strategy can lead to the vision of the company, and ultimately the senior management and leadership of the company, being discredited.

Exercise 8: Market entry problems

Examine the problems that have occurred in the management of your company's international operations. This exercise will help you develop a perspective on the approaches used by your company and whether you see them as effective or not.

Please tick the following points in an attempt to order your thinking:

1 What entry strategy is your company using at the moment?
   ❑ manufacturing
   ❑ licensing
   ❑ franchising
   ❑ contract manufacture
   ❑ direct investment
   ❑ strategic alliances
   ❑ competitive alliances
   ❑ joint ventures
   ❑ exporting
   ❑ knowledge agreements

2 How effective has the implementation of your company's chosen entry strategy/ies been?
   ❑ very good
   ❑ average
   ❑ poor
   ❑ a disaster

3 On what basis have you made this decision?

4 What would influence your company to change its market entry strategy in the future? Any or all of these:
- ❏ poor sales
- ❏ low market share
- ❏ lack of customer responsiveness
- ❏ ineffective distribution
- ❏ lack of market analysis
- ❏ unavailable resources

Comments:

5 Which of the market entry strategies are open to you to use?
- ❏ manufacturing
- ❏ licensing
- ❏ franchising
- ❏ contract manufacture
- ❏ direct investment
- ❏ strategic alliances
- ❏ competitive alliances
- ❏ joint ventures
- ❏ exporting
- ❏ knowledge agreements

6 How does your company achieve the right match between the company and the business environment?
- ❏ detailed market research
- ❏ use of extensive modelling systems
- ❏ continuous monitoring of the competitive environment
- ❏ market intelligence
- ❏ employee ideas and feedback

WHAT ARE THE CHOICES OPEN TO YOU?

When the last chapter concluded you may have decided on the information requirements for your business.

Let's review the choices open to you when considering an appropriate market entry strategy. There are many choices open to managers considering the market entry strategy most appropriate for their company. Some of the descriptions used by managers to outline their market entry strategies are quite confusing, particularly to a new international manager. Companies may use different terms to describe the same activity within a company, and one area that is particularly confusing is the use of the term 'alliance', which seems to have become a generic term in business circles. The term 'partnership' would seem to describe many of the concepts used under the term 'alliance'.

The key questions that managers will have in their minds when making a choice of market entry strategy are as follows:

- ■ Why do some market entry strategies work in some markets and not in others?
- ■ Why do some companies have different approaches to the same marketplace?

The answers to these two straightforward questions will form the basis of the market entry strategy to be used by your company.

The aim is not necessarily to find the most complex market entry strategy but rather to develop the most sensible entry strategy configuration for your company.

Exercise 9: Market entry choice

Consider an exercise based on the hotel and catering industry:

- ■ target market – Malta
- ■ product – luxury hotels
- ■ company – international hotel group
- ■ market information – extensive
- ■ company competencies – quality brand
  excellent staff
  strong financial support
  management style that
  encourages risk-taking
- ■ market entry choice –

You may be able to think of more options available to this company but for the moment let's consider the following:

- franchising;
- direct construction of the hotel;
- strategic alliance.

Each option will have a series of advantages and disadvantages but you have to make a decision. Which one would you choose and why?

Some of the advantages and disadvantages of each choice are shown below.

	Advantages	Disadvantages
Franchising	Commitment of owner-manager	Dilution of control
	Speed of market entry	Training
	Spread risk of investment	Ensuring uniformity
Direct construction	Control	High level of cost
	Management	Time
	Quality	Long-term commitment
Strategic alliance	Share risk	Share secrets
	Matching expertise	Loyalty
	Political support	Potentially less income

ALTERNATIVE MARKET ENTRY STRATEGIES

The choices available to an international business manager are very similar to the choices available to a military person considering the choice of weapons that can be used in any type of situation. The secret of success is knowing which weapon to use in each particular situation. The market entry strategy will be successful only if you choose the right weapon to match your overall strategy.

Let's examine some of the alternatives open to the international business manager.

Exporting

This is often the first choice of many small businesses and manufacturing concerns. It is often the first choice of many business people because of the speed of access it provides and because of the benefits of having an agent that understands your product and is ready to market and distribute it with enthusiasm. The selection of the agent will be considered in more detail, but the selection procedure is very similar to any selection procedure in that you will have detailed criteria that need to be fulfilled before you will consider the applicant any further.

Manufacturing

The choice of manufacturing is open to many companies but it does require a high level of initial investment in manufacturing facilities. The level of commitment is also a concern for the senior management team of the company entering the new market. If you choose to manufacture your product in the target market, you cannot easily leave that market without a great deal of pain and anguish. The benefits of manufacturing are clear: you become part of the business infrastructure of the target market and enjoy the benefits of location and responsiveness to the customer.

Direct investment

Share-ownership of particular sectors of the economy is one method of gaining influence in a market. Recent examples have been the move to America of the Japanese, who have invested very heavily in businesses in the UK and America, the most famous example being direct investment in the American movie industry, which had mixed success. It may be that investment by the Japanese in the movie industry is the classic mistake made by many:

thinking that they understand a business that they have no experience of running. A more successful example of direct investment is the French water companies investing in the UK utilities sector. This investment has been a success because of the level of understanding that the French business people have of the industry and of the problems and opportunities that exist when it is managed.

Strategic alliances

The strategic alliance is increasingly common, particularly as companies start to contract out specialist functions. One key to the success of a strategic alliance is being able to develop a sense of mutual respect and trust which can underpin a mutual series of benefits and expectations about the success of the new strategic alliance. Another key aspect is commitment towards the new venture from all parties involved in the alliance. Flexibility and compatibility are important and need to be assessed before the alliance is formally structured to start. The chance that different business cultures will exist in the companies that form the alliance is highly probable and this difference needs to be managed effectively. The strategic alliance may be based on a clear understanding of the need for an effective distribution network to be established along the supply chain. The strategic alliance provides companies with an opportunity to exploit the partnership for profit.

Joint ventures

The whole concept of entering into a joint venture with another organization is increasingly attractive for a variety of companies. It may be the only choice open to an international manager because the government of the target market may have legislated to prevent you entering a market unless you have commenced a joint venture agreement with a home-based company. For example, this is the case in Cyprus.

Joint ventures may provide your company with an easy way of gaining market access to what may traditionally have been difficult terrain to operate in. This market access may be provided by the fact that you are now part of a joint venture, or it could be that because of the unity of your company competencies you can successfully gain market access to a previously difficult market.

Another reason for the success of joint ventures could be that the combination of your company's competencies and the competencies of your partner may enable you to take advantage of a market opportunity that would have been inaccessible in the past. For example, your company may have a very well-known brand name and product range and when these are combined with the expertise in marketing and technology of your partner they make a winning team that can beat the competition.

A reason often cited by companies for using joint ventures is that an organization can share risks with its partner. The sharing of risks is a factor which runs through any discussion on market entry strategies, and the structure of a joint venture allows these risks to be shared. The sharing of risks is included in the concern not only for operational or marketing costs but also for the sharing of research and development costs. Joint ventures may enable companies to manage innovation processes much more effectively.

Joint ventures also have the advantage that they increase awareness of the marketplace and company credibility in the market. Many potential investors will view the development of an effective joint venture as a competent and positive strategic move by the organization.

Licensing

Licensing is another method of market entry which tends to be very popular in the fast-moving consumer goods sector and is a recognized method of market entry for companies wishing to gain access to previously difficult markets. The whole approach of licensing allows companies to take a percentage of the profits from a product but without having direct responsibility for production matters. There is often low capital risk and low resource commitment when using the licensing approach to market entry.

An international company can gain information on product and competitors' performance at very little cost by monitoring the behaviour of its products or services through the company which has the license to produce the product. An added advantage could be the distribution network of the licensee, which may already be very well established and ready to take the new product quickly into the marketplace. The distribution of the product may also assist the delivery times and levels of quality of service to the end-user.

This approach has a series of disadvantages, particularly the disclosure of knowledge and information concerning how the product is produced, the creation of a possible future competitor for your company and lack of control over the licensee range of operations. As stated earlier, a company tends to learn from a particular market by being as closely involved in that market as possible, and the licensing option tends to offer a passive interaction with the market. Probably the most difficult aspect of operating through a licensing agreement is your ability to organize the licensee operations and to come to terms with the fact that someone else plays a major role in the success or otherwise of your company.

Franchising

Since the early 1980s this approach to business development and market entry strategy has been growing in importance, not only with the well-established and famous franchising companies such as McDonalds, Dunkin Donuts and Hertz Car Rentals, but now with well-established retailing groups such as Marks & Spencer.

The use of this method of market entry is normally associated with high levels of growth and is used by companies to gain rapid and comprehensive market entry. It is often used by companies when local knowledge is lacking, and it is prevalent in the consumer sector of the economy.

Consortia

The term 'consortium' is normally used when a group of companies combine their knowledge and expertise to enter a particular market and to exploit the advantages gained by an amalgamation of competencies. Consortia, or consortiums, are often used to allow large engineering projects to take place and to be effectively managed. Each consortium may be led by a recognized group or company to provide potential investors with a focal point to understand the nature of the investment opportunity.

JOINT DEVELOPMENT

Joint development and partnerships are certainly the way forward for many companies. This trend started in earnest in the early 1990s and looks set to progress quite rapidly, led by a host of international businesses, including British Airways, Rolls-Royce and Sony. Emphasis is placed on the need to share costs and technology in the search for competitive advantage.

Let's consider the example of Rolls-Royce Aeroengines, who in 1990 were setting a fast pace for the expansion of the company in terms of its international markets, based on a series of partnerships and collaborations.

At the beginning of the 1990s Rolls-Royce Aeroengines had a series of partnerships with companies involved in the production of their products. Below, I have outlined the range of products they had in production during the period, as well as the countries that were involved in research, development and final production. I have also listed some of the companies involved in the partnership process. The company views partnerships as the only legitimate way forward in terms of containing research costs, controlling the time involved in development and implementing a successful market entry strategy.

Their products included the following:

- Tornado fighter engine;
- International aeroengine;
- Tay small airliner engine;
- Trent high-thrust airliner engine;
- Eurojet fighter aircraft – Eurojet 200.

There were a number of countries involved in the production of these products, including Germany, the USA, Italy, Japan, Sweden, France and Spain. The companies involved in the range of products being produced by the company included MTU, Fiat, Pratt & Whitney, Japan Aero Engine Company, Volvo, Alfa Romeo, BMW, Hurel Dubois, Hispano Sulsa, Kawasaki, IHI and ITP.

Exercise 10: Interdependence of international businesses

The above example illustrates the complex nature of many international businesses and demonstrates the interdependence of many businesses in the international business environment.

Let's look at your organization.

■ List the main products and services offered by your company:

■ List the products and services that are being developed by your company:

■ List any links your company has with suppliers in terms of research, development or electronic data interchange systems:

■ Examine the interdependencies between all three of these areas of business activity and make some notes for future discussion:

Conclusions:

This analysis should enable you to draw some interesting conclusions about the range of interdependencies and linkages within your business and the effect this is likely to have on the choice of market entry strategy for the future.

You can start to ask the correct questions of your business and your partners' and competitors' activities:

■ What approaches to market entry are being adopted by your competitors?

■ How are your partners developing future strategic positions?

■ Are there any lessons you can learn from your partners?

■ What is the future direction of interdependency between your company and its partners?

EVALUATING STRATEGIC OPTIONS

The evaluation of the strategic options open to your company can to a certain extent be based on experience and the success or failure of your competitors. The international company has to evaluate all the options available and not be swayed by the most popular methods of the moment that may be considered by its competitors.

The development of company criteria for market entry assessment is also crucial and needs to be based on a long-term view of the future of the company in that market. Another consideration is the need to align the long-term interests of market entry with the long-term business strategy and profitability of the business. The final consideration is the likelihood of entry into this market providing your company with any long-term opportunities in similar or associated markets.

Senior management needs to lead the work on the design of the criteria for selection of new market opportunities and this will involve a concerted effort to secure the correct level of resources, in terms of people, technology and finance, to take full advantage of the emerging market. The link between the marketing planning and strategic planning departments is crucial in gaining an understanding of the market and the impact the entry strategy will have on the long-term strategy of the international business. Senior management can also play a role in ensuring that the key functions of the business cooperate and work towards the long-term success of the business.

The implementation of the options available to the international company is crucial to its success and can be enhanced by the correct allocation of time and resources to the new project. Many market entry strategies can fail because of a lack of senior management foresight and strategic management of the whole process of implementation.

4 *Developing a sustainable competitive advantage*

The competitive advantage within a company can be compared to the star player in a football team. The development and nurturing of the star enables the team to be successful and to secure a strong position in the already competitive arena. In this chapter we will investigate four key areas which are important to the development of success. They include the need to understand the major influences on competition, maintaining the pressures to improve, the role of strategic planning and the aim of continuous analysis of the competitive environment.

The development of a sustainable competitive advantage is probably the most difficult task facing an international business manager. The word 'sustainable' is now being used a great deal in connection with competitive advantage and is defined as 'able to be maintained or prolonged'. Competitive advantage can be defined as the development of a superior position in a market by offering the customers a series of benefits which motivate them to purchase one company's product or service instead of the competitor's. Many companies believe that unless you can develop a competitive advantage in new international markets you are beaten before you even start.

This chapter will discuss these basic concepts and seek to examine the importance of strategic planning and competitive analysis in developing a position within a marketplace. A model will be used to show the levels at which competitive advantage is possible and the need for creative thinking in formulating and implementing competitive strategies.

The competitive strategy that your company has developed may not be changing quite so rapidly as that of the competition because of your position in the sector or marketplace. For example, if your company is a market follower with limited resources it will be very difficult suddenly to challenge for leadership in a market let alone to become a market challenger.

Case outline: Sony

Sony have developed a competitive strategy based on integrating the hardware and software businesses in the electronics industry, particularly in the field of audio-visuals. The hardware and software for the product are closely linked by means of a technical standard called the format. The company leads the development of a new generation of standards which form the basis of the format and assist the company in restructuring the competitive environment of the industry. The success of this competitive strategy is centred on the need simultaneously to attract the competition into the industry and push out other competitors from the sector.

For a successful outcome the following must be true:

■ many manufacturers offering hardware and software products must be basing their products on the format;
■ a coalition of manufacturers using the same format must include the major players in the industry;
■ hardware and software must be supplied to the market continuously and reliably.

Other factors which are important are cost advantages, a high level of market share, the ability to influence strongly the entry barriers to the sector and the ability to integrate vertically and horizontally.

Sony have utilized this approach in the compact-disc player market, for instance when the company introduced the Discman into the market. The result was an increase in customer demand and market leadership. With the new generation of products there were few companies that could compete because of the need for new recording equipment. The audio-visual sector became very capital intensive and competitors who could not sustain the high levels of investment purchased the key components or recording systems from Sony to maintain their product lines. A change in the competitive nature of the industry had taken place in a short and significant period.

David Francis, in his book *Step-By-Step Competitive Strategy* (1994), defines competitive advantage as 'the bundle of advantages which impels a customer to choose your firm's products rather than another's'. He supports this definition by stating that the theory of competitive strategy is based on the customer's perception of value and that the concept of value differs from one customer to another.

These two points are very useful in trying to understand the challenges facing international businesses in their search for competitive advantage. The definition used by Francis is particularly good because it focuses the attention of managers on the importance of impelling the customer to choose their products or services from a range of available choices. The word 'impel' is interesting because it implies that customers cannot help themselves when choosing your product or service; they choose your product as if by second nature and without thinking.

The other key phrase is 'bundle of benefits', which implies that the eventual offering to the customer could be quite complex or haphazard but that if the customer is happy with the product or service that is what counts. The bundle of benefits could be linked to the performance of the product or the additional level of service which is provided by the company.

The competitive strategy has to be clear and needs to match the desires of the customer as closely as possible.

Let's also consider the example of a European airline which invited a project team to examine the company and to recommend changes to the organization which would have long-term effects on its competitive position in the industry. The project team consisted of individuals who had expertise in the areas of operations, marketing, finance and logistics, etc.; they knew a great deal about the industry and its likely direction in the future. The airline was government-owned and considered a difficult industry to manage by many experts. It would require a radical approach to change the competitive position of this company in what was becoming an increasingly cut-throat operating environment.

The project commenced with a very detailed study examining the following areas of company policy, strategy and operations:

- distribution;
- cost of operations;
- processes and systems;
- people costs;
- possible trade union reaction;
- government subsidy levels;
- logistics;
- marketing strategy;

■ financial structure;
■ supplier network.

The report was then prepared and considered carefully, but no action was taken. This may have been because of the political sensitivity and overall difficulties involved in managing the change successfully. It could have been because the timing of such a massive change was just not right and would have involved a great deal of heartache for everyone involved.

This may have been fair justification for no action being taken by the senior management team of this organization. The issue is really about how the competitive environment is affected by such actions or indeed by lack of action.

THE MAJOR INFLUENCES ON SUSTAINING COMPETITIVE ADVANTAGE IN YOUR COMPANY

The competitive environment of an international company is often very complex and difficult to understand. This may be because the threat of competition may come from any part of the world. The traditional competitors of some companies are changing, both in terms of their structure as a company and their origin. The struggle for many senior managers of international businesses is to identify the development of the competition and then to second-guess its competitive strategy. The source of competitive threat will vary and could be in any part of the globe. The need in many companies is therefore to keep the competitive advantage of the company as relevant to existing markets as possible.

The influences on your company during its drive to develop a sustainable competitive advantage can be shown in Figure 4.7.

Continuous drive towards improvements in operating systems

This requires a consistent push towards improving each operating system within the company. It could centre on a total quality management or competitive benchmarking programme, which could be used to focus the attention of every company employee throughout the world on the need to improve on a consistent basis. The content of the programme could focus on the competition and the processes they have in place, or it could be a concerted effort

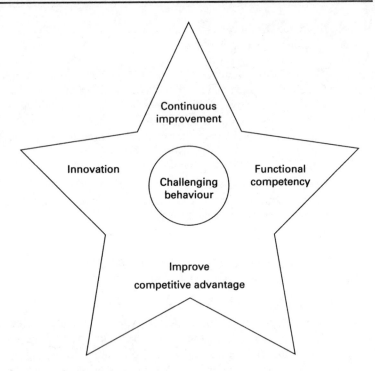

Figure 4.7 Competitive star

by the company to raise standards above the competition and eventually beat them.

Innovation strategies that provide new concepts for products and services

The corporate culture needs to facilitate innovation and promote it at every opportunity throughout the company. The innovation strategy may be a detailed document which is clearly understood by everyone in the organization, or it could be a series of new product development targets used by the company to increase the level of growth within the portfolio of businesses. The focus on business development could also be a method used by the company to diversify its commercial options as a business, for example to decrease the emphasis on acquisitions, increase the level of collaborative projects focusing on research and development or concentrate on organic growth as a means of building the business.

Making improvements throughout the range of activities in the company

Each function within the company could be looking to make improvements in its contribution to the competitive advantage of the business. These could be improvements in the strategic thinking of the business managers, particularly in terms of logistical strategy, or improvements in market research information and strategy implementation. Alternatively it might mean the search for enhancements to human resource management strategy in training and development, reward systems and career structures. In addition, changes and improvements in production methods could be made and systems set up to encourage increases in company performance.

Challenging the expected mode of behaviour in the company

It can be productive to develop a restlessness inside the company which challenges the expected type of behaviour within the company. This restlessness would need to become part of the company culture and be led and supported by senior management behaviour throughout the company. Challenging the expected norms of behaviour would be necessary to stimulate the company to adapt to the changing circumstances of the marketplace and to stop a complacent attitude becoming the accepted way of managing the company.

Attempting to upgrade the sources of advantage in the company

The sources of advantage need to be upgraded and the starting point for most companies is to identify their distinct competencies and seek to build on their success. Competencies may exist in a range of company activities, including a high level of expertise in manufacturing, expertise in logistics, management or marketing skills, financial strength of the company and brand management experience. These competencies can be upgraded by careful management and a recognition by senior management that the resources required to move the company forward have to be made available to the key areas of the business.

In developing an approach to managing and maintaining a sustainable competitive advantage, an international company has to be very effective at assessing trends within its chosen marketplace and be sufficiently aware of the competitors' strategies to counter-act any perceived threat. This requires an imaginative approach to strategic thinking and a great deal of information on the future direction of the market. This must be allied to the acceptance that pressures to maintain a competitive advantage have to be sought.

MAINTAINING PRESSURES TO IMPROVE

Maintaining the pressures to improve and develop a competitive advantage requires an understanding of the markets in which your company operates and a realization that competitiveness does not necessarily come from dominating a market and squeezing out all competition. This can be seen in the Sony company, where their entry into the compact disc market enabled them to enter the components business. Today the compact disc is an important product for Sony, not only in final assembly but also in key components.

This understanding will prepare the company for the changes that may take place at any time in the marketplace. The search for competitive advantage is very similar to the training soldiers may receive during peacetime: soldiers have to remain prepared at all times and keep themselves up to date with the new methods being used in their area of expertise, ready to compete at any time. The international business may not find an environment as threatening as the military example but the principles are the same. The international business may not know when the competitor is likely to strike and must be ahead in terms of business methods and thinking (see Figure 4.8).

Look for sophisicated buyers of your products and services

One method of trying to stay ahead of the competition is to seek out more sophisicated purchasers of your products and services. This strategy needs to be allied to an understanding of the buying process that your key customers use when making a buying deci-sion. The sophisicated buyer will be more demanding on the skills and knowledge of your business and maintain the pressure to innovate. The sophisicated buyer will expect higher levels of customer service and technological support from the business.

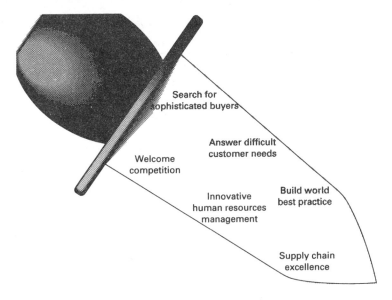

Search for
sophisticated buyers

Answer difficult
customer needs

Welcome
competition

Innovative
human resources
management

Build world
best practice

Supply chain
excellence

Figure 4.8 Staying sharp

Answer the difficult needs of customers

Listening to the difficult and complex needs of the customer can
have a dual benefit for the international business: your business
may be perceived, on the one hand, as a dynamic business ahead in
certain areas of technology and, on the other, as a business which
wants to work alongside its customers to form a working partnership. This approach would place your business in a strong position
to gain the benefits of partnership, which seems to be the most
appropriate manner in which to gain a competitive advantage in
many of today's international markets.

Build on world best standards of quality

Quality standards must be met and then exceeded by the international business searching for a way to maintain the pressures for
competitive advantage. National standards must be beaten and the
successful international business must play a role in setting international standards of quality for the industry. The approach to
quality can benefit the organization through the introduction of
quality-control methods which promote excellent quality of customer service and product development.

Develop excellence along the supply chain

Managing the set of customer/supplier relationships can be defined as supply chain management and this is becoming a major area of activity for the most successful international businesses. It involves the management of a range of relationships, from that with the initial or basic suppliers to your business right through to that with the end-user. The chain of contacts between these two groups requires successful management and may include component suppliers, purchasing departments, marketing function, technical support, buyers and end-users. Supply chain management can be an important weapon in focusing management effort on the need to look for improvements by taking a fresh look at the totality of the business.

Welcome competition into your sector

This may seem to be a strange request for any business, because most businesses tend to spend their whole existence fighting the competition, but the basic logic behind welcoming competition into your business sector is that it maintains the pressures on your organization to improve. The need for competition in a business sector is sometimes unavoidable as governments search for new and different methods of broadening the competitive base of their industrial and commercial sectors. An attitude amongst senior managers which promotes competition can lead to a more dynamic approach to the international marketplace through the acceptance that change and competition are always threatening the future of the business.

Adopt innovative human resource management strategies

The adoption of international strategies for the management of human resources can add competitive advantage to an international business. Training and development can be focused towards key business issues, such as new product development and improving the launch of new products into existing markets. Internal selection can be centred on making the most appropriate skills available to particular areas of need within the business as effectively as possible. The strategy for human resource management can also be geared towards providing a method of motivating and integrating the companies who operate on a temporary partnership basis with the international business.

Build on world best practice in marketing management

Building on the best practice in marketing will enable the international business to concentrate on developing a set of shared values within the company which place the customer at the centre of company thinking. Develop a management style which provides support for marketing initiatives and a lean structure which provides an efficient and effective marketing service throughout the company. These initiatives will be supported by a clear marketing orientation throughout the company which enables people to understand market trends, segmentation and the analytical skills of marketing.

This marketing orientation will be supported by customer and competitor intelligence reports, product line profitability reports and marketing planning and control systems. These efforts will be led by a formalized vision and mission for the company, a strategic marketing plan, precise marketing objectives and a strong commitment from senior management to the successful implementation of an international marketing strategy.

All of these elements and initiatives can assist the international business in its drive towards the achievement of a sustainable competitive advantage.

Case outline: British Airways

The sustainable competitive advantage of British Airways is based on customer service and the belief that although the company carries thousands of people, it looks after the individual needs of its customers.

British Airways has changed from a company that seemed to disdain customers to one that strives to please them at every stage of the relationship. The company is not content with sustaining a competitive advantage in Europe or the Americas; its ambition is to become the first truly global airline. It has developed a competitive strategy which has focused on the setting up of alliances with other carriers around the globe. It has stakes in US Air, Quantas Airways, TAT European Airlines, Deutsche BA and American Airlines. The obvious competitive challenge for the company is to deliver consistent, high-quality service in a complex people business (difficult for one company), but it has to succeed across a group of companies. The key elements of BA's competitive advantage is differentiation, value for money, research and customer retention – to go beyond the function and compete on the basis of providing an experience.

THE ROLE OF STRATEGIC PLANNING

Strategic planning has an important role to play in developing a competitive advantage for any international business. The function assists in the development of strategic plans but, perhaps more importantly, monitors the implementation of a successful strategic planning process within the company.

Strategic planning has changed dramatically since its early development in the 1970s. Having survived the original flaws in design, it has evolved into a viable system of strategic management. There has been a series of notable changes in the profession and a shift in responsibility from staff to line management, decentralization of strategic planning to business units and increased attention to changing markets, technology and the competitive environment. Planning systems are more sophisicated and a greater emphasis is being placed on techniques such as scenario planning, total quality management and benchmarking.

The process of strategic planning is much more sensitive to the uncertainties and unknowns of many markets than in the past. More emphasis on organizational and cultural issues and on the implementation of strategy is being considered by strategists of many international companies. There is a clear recognition that people, corporate values, motivation and organizational behaviour are crucial to the success of international companies.

Case outline: British Gas

If we look at the example of British Gas plc, we can see that the company believes that its competitive advantage centres on the ability to develop expertise in all areas of its business, from the drill bit to the burner tip. A complete understanding of the industrial sector, 'The Gas Chain', supports this level of expertise and this is further reinforced by a strong reputation in the international marketplace. This competitive advantage can be summarized as:

- an understanding of the dynamics of the industry;
- high levels of industry expertise;
- strong reputation or brand name in the marketplace.

The company was privatized by the UK Government in the 1980s, and since this took place it has focused very heavily on its expansion into the international marketplace.

Another focal point within the company has been the change in organizational culture that has taken place over the last ten years and which in essence is still continuing. British Gas has a strong belief that the cultural change that has taken place in the company has formed a critical part in the continuous drive towards a sustainable competitive advantage. Another aspect of business strategy which will support the move towards a sustainable competitive advantage is the increased use of joint ventures, alliances and collaborations. The business is becoming much more complex and managers are expected to act and think internationally.

It would therefore appear that the competitive advantage of the company is based around five key elements, namely:

- an understanding of the dynamics of the industry;
- high levels of industry expertise;
- a strong reputation or brand name in the marketplace;
- a change in organizational culture;
- increased use of joint ventures, alliances and collaborations.

These sources of sustainable competitive advantage within the company are focused on a range of issues, not just on driving down and controlling the costs in the business. These include:

- strategic planning skills;
- brand management;
- technological skills;
- corporate culture;
- partnership strategies.

These elements need to be consistently reinforced by the strategic management of the company. This reinforcement can be supported by a dynamic approach to business development which takes place on a worldwide basis and is organized by the strategic planning function via the country managers within each region of the company.

The competitive strategy is ultimately set by the Board of the company but it is implemented by the country managers throughout the organization. The strategic planning function of the company has a 'carrot and stick' approach to developing ideas throughout the company on how an effective competitive advantage can be sustained and market opportunities exploited. The carrot and stick approach takes the form of inviting ideas from employees in the international sections of the business and rewarding good strategic ideas with the correct level of funding to enable the projects to commence.

The strategic planners act as facilitators within the business who assist the individual country managers to think deeply about the key issues facing the company. The strategic planning function attempts to assist in the implementation of some of these ideas on a continuous basis. This support from the centre of the organization provides the individual managers with a feeling of confidence and builds on their previous experience of strategic management. The aim of this approach is to build a flexible and informal company which can adapt to the changing marketplace in a responsive and positive manner.

Business development ideas come from the individual business units and are presented to the Board of the company at regular strategic reviews. These reviews are used as opportunities to consider the competitive advantage of the company and to monitor the implementation of the competitive strategy of the company.

The impact on competitive advantage is seen at two levels, as shown in Figure 4.9. The first level is the focus on the need to sustain competitive advantage; the second is the focus on constant improvement.

CONTINUOUS COMPETITIVE ANALYSIS

A project team or a specific department – namely, strategic planning or marketing – could be responsible for conducting a continuous analysis of the competitive environment. Continuous analysis of the competition could be based on a detailed analysis of the elements in the competitive environment outlined below.

Industry analysis

Industry analysis is a detailed overview of the changes and developments taking place in your sector of the international economy at a given time. Industry analysis should be able to tell you the key factors that are motivating the companies in your sector of the industry; how the forces of change have changed over the last few years and what new pressures will exist in your industry in the

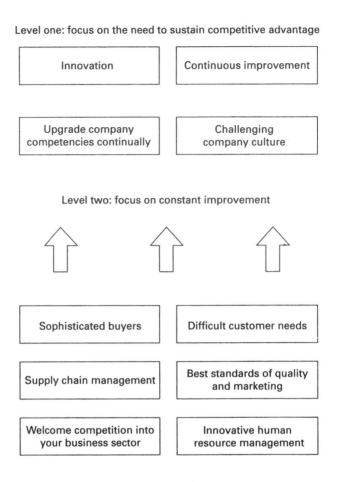

Figure 4.9 Two levels of impact on competitive advantage

coming years; who the fastest growth companies in your sector are and how difficult it would be to challenge the successful companies. Technological developments, industry structure and competitive changes can be identified through industry analysis. Perhaps the key factors which are likely to affect your analysis of the industry are changes regarding the customer and how the demand for the products or services within your sector is likely to change.

Industry mapping

Industry mapping is a useful method of comparing the size of each company within a particular sector. The basic idea is to identify the size of each company in relation to the others, in order to spot growing companies and identify the level of dominance of the leading players in the industry. This method is useful for spotting developments and differences between companies and as a snapshot of the present position of an industry.

Identifying the critical success factors

The critical success factors that enable companies to succeed within your sector can be identified. These factors could include a location which gives you access to a range of new and developing markets or regions. In addition, the critical success factor could be access to distribution networks within your target market which provide you with a lead over the competition. The critical success factors need to be carefully identified and analysed before your company enters a new market because a lack of understanding can place your company at a competitive disadvantage when attempting to secure a strategic position within a market.

Competitor profiling

The key competitors within your sector can be profiled to gain a clear view of their positions within the target market. Competitor profiling can be based on any range of factors, such as:

- financial structure and viability;
- distribution network;
- management expertise;
- manufacturing capability;
- marketing competencies;
- industry achievements;
- market share;

- technological leadership;
- brand awareness within the marketplace;
- customer loyalty.

Special competitor studies

Competitor profiling can take place within an industry on a frequent basis, but a company may also request that a special competitor profile be taken of one or two key competitors within the target sector. This may be because these competitors are viewed as threatening to the success of your international expansion or because they require detailed analysis to identify weaknesses in their overall strategy as a company. The special competitor studies can take the form of a detailed report from the strategic planning or marketing function and could be presented to the Board of the company during a detailed strategic review of the future of the business in its existing and potential international markets.

Analysis of the value chain

The value chain, as discussed by Dave Francis, is shown in the twelve-box model and is illustrated in Figure 4.10.[1] The initial aspect that will concern you is is the term 'margin' on the right of the illustration. This represents the economic motive of the company, which is to add value faster than it adds business costs.

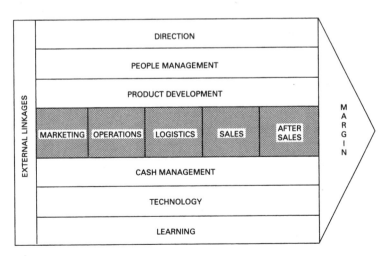

Figure 4.10 The value chain

In many companies there is a complex relationship between these twelve elements: the five areas in the centre of the illustration drive the business forward and are supported by the seven additional aspects of the business, such as direction, people management and product development.[2]

Competitor benchmarking

Benchmarking is an objective and comparative evaluation of organizational structure, cost and performance using specific indicators established through direct research among a representative group of competing companies. The process of competitor benchmarking enables your company to gain a concrete understanding of the competition, generate new ideas of proven practices and technology and develop a high level of commitment within the company. It can help you solve real productivity problems based on industry best practice and assist in the development of superior performance throughout the company. The company's goals can also be viewed as more credible and proactive and possibly lead to an industry leading position for your company. Benchmarking is a valuable tool for comparisons and a logical step for enhancing performance measurement and target-setting.

The benchmarking process is based on four key stages:

1 Planning: What? Who? Data?
2 Analysis: measure; trends.
3 Integration: communicate; goals.
4 Action: plan; implement; recalibrate.

The decisions to be made focus on the data to be collected, the comparison problems and the need to understand industry trends. The outcomes of the competitive benchmarking process need to be communicated to the correct functions within the company and the benchmarking goals need to be integrated into the existing improvement programmes within the company by setting 'best practice' goals.

Exercise 11: Competitive information

Changes in the business environment have forced even our most stable international companies to change. The key driving force behind many of the changes affecting these companies has been the unpredictable nature of the competitive threat. In response to the new pressures in the competitive environment, managers find it difficult to access the information required to deal with the external threat. Competitive information enables you to understand the response of the competition before they take action.

Outline the areas of competitive information which your company has direct access to:

Answer the following questions:
- ❑ Does the information help you understand current competitor strategy?
- ❑ Does the information help you understand long-term changes to the market?
- ❑ Does the information help you understand the need for increased resources to compete?
- ❑ Does the information describe culture?
- ❑ Does the information allow you to make assumptions?
- ❑ Does the information help you understand the impact of the information on the future direction of the business?

Exercise review:

You may find that this exercise leaves some major gaps in the understanding of your company's business environment. Spend thirty minutes, preferably with colleagues, constructing an action plan which can plug the gaps in your understanding of the competitive environment.

Sustaining a competitive advantage can only be achieved by aiming to manage your company effectively so that this can lead to superior performance. There is no secret formula that can be followed to achieve success, but certainly the following ten factors will place your company in a strong position:

1 Develop a comprehensive and clear strategy on how you are going to achieve competitive advantage before considering the tactics required to seize competitive advantage.
2 Ensure that the marketing and operational functions within the business collaborate successfully.
3 Instill a marketing orientation throughout the company.
4 Design an organizational structure that is focused on your markets.
5 Continually scan the environment to spot opportunities and prepare the organization against threats to success.
6 Access information and feed the key issues to strategic thinkers within the company.
7 Develop skills and knowledge that add value to the future of the business.
8 Systemize the business processes within the company.
9 Prioritize the international objectives of your business.
10 Develop an international company culture and management style.

Creative thinking is needed in the search for competitive advantage in many companies, and senior management have to be driving the process of change if any improvement is to be achieved. Companies will always compete by providing superior products at a price that the market will stand, but they must be aware of the fact that it is customers, as well as competitors, who define a company's ultimate success. In the search for competitive advantage it may be helpful to improve a company's competence in analysing the competition, especially in the areas of innovation and research and development. Anticipation of competitors' responses is important for many international companies, and this needs to be supported by a review and improvement in management competence to ensure success.

5 Organization and management

This chapter will examine the difficulties involved in placing, developing and motivating the right people for international businesses. We will also look at the type of organizational structure required in the international businesses of the 1990s. People and the organizational structures they inhabit have rarely been at the top of the agenda when senior managers are formulating international business strategy. Increasingly, however, there is a recognition that people can play a major role in enhancing the competitive advantage of an international business. In the previous chapter we discussed some of the key elements needed to build an effective competitive advantage and witnessed how the correct use of people, organizational structures and systems can strengthen your competitive advantage in the international marketplace.[1]

We have discussed sustainable competitive advantage in some detail and your work has provided you with the confidence to achieve your strategy, if only on paper. If you were to ask any military strategist about the importance of people, management and organization, they would reply that these are indeed central to the success of any military campaign.

When you discuss the success of international businesses with strategic planners of major international businesses they will state that people are crucial to ensuring the success or failure of an international business strategy. They may elaborate on that statement by commenting that people are required to deliver the international strategy and that good and effective people are difficult to find and are often limited in number. They may also state that the human resource management strategy has to be an integral part of the overall corporate strategy of the company.

The question of integration is fundamental to the success of your international business strategy and is often the major area of complaint of senior human resource managers in international businesses. Human resource managers would argue that people and the manner in which they are managed, motivated, structured and rewarded have to be integrated into the overall corporate strategy of the company.

Case outline: ICL/Fujitsu

Selecting someone who can act globally

The basic philosophy underpinning the strategic approach to selection is that it is the people within the company who are responsible for implementing the international business strategy of any company. A clear understanding has to be gained of the overall direction of the business and the resultant human resource needs of the organization. The key skills required by ICL/Fujitsu include the ability to cope with rapid corporate change, a focus on new product development, concentration on quality management and the acceptance of the concept of interdependence.

ICL/Fujitsu recognize that the international marketplace is becoming quite fragmented and that it requires a different approach towards business development than that previously considered by the company. Each person in the business has to be able to spot business opportunities, and the selection procedure is based on recruiting people who can listen to the needs of the customer and integrate resources to produce action.

The company focus is on the following behavioural traits:

- tolerance of ambiguous situations more readily;
- autonomy and freedom in everyday decision-making;
- enjoyment in taking calculated risks;
- adaptability to change;
- resistance to conformity.

These traits are welcome in the company but problems have been identified during the introduction of new methods of working. These problems have focused on activities important to the success of international operations, such as communication, delegation and reward and incentive systems. The emphasis of the selection process at the company is centred on the desire for increased flexibility in the employees' response to customer needs and a drive to reach higher levels of energy throughout the international operations of the company.

Exercise 12: Effective people management

Let's consider your own company and the key questions that you need to ask relating to how your company utilizes people effectively in its drive to achieve competitive advantage.

■ Outline the key elements of your company's sustainable competitve advantage.

■ What role do people play in the development of this advantage?

■ Identify the areas of human resource expertise in your company.

■ Identify which actions need to be taken to implement an effective human resource management strategy.

■ How can these organizational changes be implemented in the short, medium and long term?

1 short term

2 medium term

3 long term

Exercise review:

You may find that your thinking focused on particular systems used in the management of human resources within your company, including the following:

❑ development opportunities
❑ recruitment policies
❑ career systems
❑ incentives and recognition
❑ organizational structures
❑ expenditure on training and development
❑ confusion over the role of human resource management

ADVANTAGES OF EFFECTIVE PEOPLE MANAGEMENT

The advantages of effective people management are difficult for line managers to appreciate because there are a large number of intangibles to be considered; for example:

■ How can you show that there is a direct cost/benefit to employing additional management expertise?
■ How can you prove that your new organizational structure is providing the payback you originally envisioned?
■ Does management development have a real impact on the success or otherwise of international businesses?
■ Can you find a direct link between your reward and recognition system and improvements in performance and motivation amongst the sales teams?

There is little doubt that not having the right people at the right time in the right place can lead to failure in terms of international business. The changing nature of organizations and how they relate to the marketplace are the key factors to consider in this chapter. There is a clear change taking place in organizations throughout the world, in that they are moving away from the bureaucratic structures of the past and towards a more flexible organizational structure which is very responsive to the changing needs of the international customer.

In the previous chapter we discussed the need for organizations to become marketing-oriented in their search for a sustainable competitive advantage, as well as the strong reliance on people and how they are managed in ensuring that marketing orientation takes place.

Customers are becoming more demanding and sophisticated in their requirements, and the pressure from the customer is focusing companies' attention on the best methods of organization to meet those requirements.

The changes taking place in many organizations are away from centralization and towards decentralization. Whether or not there is a cyclical pattern to these changes is difficult to predict, but certainly the trend is towards delegation and customer responsiveness (see Figure 5.11).

Research has shown that executives in the centralized departments of companies have very similar criticisms to the managers within the subsidiaries. Problems identified by headquarters executives include:

- lack of qualified international people;
- lack of strategic thinking and long-range planning in the subsidiaries of the company;
- lack of marketing expertise at subsidiary level in the company;
- too little communication;
- insufficient use of headquarters marketing expertise;
- restricted headquarters control of subsidiaries.

On the other hand, subsidiary managers tend to focus on the following problems, which they believe impinge on the successful implementation of the international business plans of the company:

CENTRALIZATION	DECENTRALIZATION
increased coordination	avoidance of top management emphasis
broad company perspective at the top	increase in motivation
balance between functions	development of managers
economies of scale	rapid response to change
enhancement of capability of senior people	local skills and knowledge
strong leadership	potential enhancement of autonomy and profit responsibility

Figure 5.11 Advantages of centralization and decentralization

- excessive headquarters control procedures;
- excessive financial and marketing constraints from the centre;
- insufficient participation of subsidiaries in product decisions;
- insensitivity of headquarters to local differences;
- shortage of useful information from headquarters;
- lack of international orientation of headquarters.

If you examine these problems you may arrive at the conclusion that the subsidiary managers require more detailed training and development to understand the strategy of the company or that the company needs to improve levels of communication between headquarters and subsidiary managers. Whatever your conclusion, the challenge for both levels of management is to minimize the risk of these problems developing into factors which have a detrimental effect on company performance.

One solution to the problems identified by both levels of management is to examine and revitalize the organizational structures being used within the company. There is a tendency in many well-established businesses to operate in a bureaucratic manner, and often the bureaucratic nature of the company can stifle innovation and business development. It is difficult to avoid some of the aspects of bureaucracy because elements of control and stability can be enhanced by using bureaucratic systems and procedures. The argument required in international business is that bureaucracy is counter-productive and that organizations need to be built around new concepts.

Case outline: IBM

In common with the rest of the IBM organization, IBM UK needed to take radical action between 1991 and 1993 to restore investor confidence and company profitability. The actions it took included the restructuring of the company into a federation of businesses, changing the management systems and increasing the focus of the management team towards customer responsiveness and quality. The company developed an approach to strategic management which complemented many of the structural changes taking place in the company. The aim of the structural and managerial changes was to stimulate an innovation culture and an awareness throughout the company of the needs of the customer. The corporate culture had to change and that change needed to evolve at the same time as the changes taking place within the organization. New approaches included the following:

■ the redefinition of the corporate mission;
■ integration of business and holding company strategies;
■ joint focus on the customer and financial performance/quality.

Changing the behaviour of many managers who had made their careers within the previous command and control structure was much more difficult than changing the organizational structure. There was a need to devolve decision-making so that it was closer to the customer to get the customer responsiveness necessary for future success.

To achieve these changes IBM adopted a structure with a small holding company and twenty-five businesses. There were three main types of business, covering product, services and industry, and they were organized in groupings or sets. These were based on earlier central staff functions, technical functions and the sales branches. There were also some shared service units which targeted all areas of the business.

Strong interdependencies developed which are now evident in many other international businesses. Single large customers would inevitably offer the same products and services as other businesses, and businesses were frequently dependent on others for their market access. The image of IBM was also dependent on all businesses adopting the same vision and values.

The role of the centre was as follows:

■ to decide the distribution of limited resources between federation members;
■ to invest in new opportunities/areas not being covered by existing businesses;
■ to disinvest in markets/systems which were no longer an integral part of the business as a whole;
■ to establish shared values and a style to bind the federation;
■ to add value by provoking strategic thinking and reviewing strategies;
■ to optimize performance by not granting licences for unattractive markets.

The greatest contribution of the new management structure and style has been in stimulating the new businesses to think as independent, cooperative entities rather than sales branches.

The aim of the change was to encourage businesses to:

- understand markets;
- understand the competition;
- define the sources of competitive advantage;
- define product offerings and market approach;
- select markets to address;
- balance long and short-term goals;
- build a coherent competitive strategy.

The results are significant and the company has seen increased revenue, profitability and competitiveness, as well as an increased understanding of the needs of the customer.

NEW CONCEPTS FOR THE FUTURE

These new concepts may focus on the network style of organization outlined in this chapter, but certainly technology and the application of technological systems will play a major role in the design of international businesses. The organization of international business has moved from an uncontrolled chaos to diversified conglomerates to focused business units. Successful international companies are developing into a collection of units with core competencies and creating a network of strategic business entities. The conglomerates of the early days of international business are being replaced by strategic networks. The new development is the move towards 'small is beautiful', and the clearest example of this is IBM, followed by ABB and even BP.

There are four basic types of network organization:

1 Internal network. Examples are ABB and Johnson & Johnson, and they operate in a very similar manner to strategic business units.
2 Diagonal network. An example is TCI, which has connections with a range of diverse organizations in the hope of exploiting synergies between interdependent markets.
3 Vertical network. The best examples are Toyota, which uses its *keiretsu* system of alliances to manage the organization, and Benetton, which uses upward and backward networks to manage the company.
4 Horizontal network. Alliances form the backbone of this example and they are usually formed to exploit technological advancements or geographical advantages in particular markets. The recent alliance between American Airlines and British Airways, set up to exploit the UK to US routes, is a notable example.

The potential would seem to be there for many companies to exploit these principles of organizational design and benefit quite substantially. The key question is often which part of the network ultimately has control over the strategic decision-making process within the network.

Let's examine some of the typical aspects to be found in both types of organization. While you are reading this section, ask yourself if you recognize your organization or an organization that you are familiar with. You may recognize many of the aspects outlined below within your company, or perhaps you have begun to witness a move away from this style of operating or at least a dramatic change in the terms used by companies.

Manager

This term has been used to describe the activities of people within companies and centres on several key skills: organizing, directing, planning and motivating. The manager has ultimate responsibility for a function or department of a company and will be part of a well-defined career structure. This is a well-understood term and one already established in many international companies as the title of choice for many individuals who have responsibility for a clearly defined part of the international business.

Internal competition

Internal competition will often be found in international businesses as the clearly defined departments or functions attempt to secure additional financing for their projects through the budgeting system of the company. Internal competition is encouraged because of the increased levels of efficiency and effectiveness that can result from direct competition for scarce company resources.

Emphasis on hierarchy

The bureaucratic organization will be built on a hierarchy of positions within the organizational structure which will feed information up the organizational tree and centre key decision-making at the top of the company. The hierarchy will have a strong reliance on control of the company's resources, and the decision-making process of the company will be based on well-understood procedures and systems that are applicable on a international basis.

Vertical communication

The communication channels of the bureaucratic international business will be established on a vertical basis, in that information will not flow across the organizational departments or functions but will tend to follow the decisions of senior management, vertical in nature and involving some feedback from departments and functions throughout the company but only through a well-designed channel of communication.

Control

Control is often the reason why bureaucratic organizations are preferred by organizational development specialists. Control is at the centre of senior management thinking in designing organizations because of the close monitoring of resources, people and decision-making that can be achieved by introducing a bureaucratic approach to the design of the international company. Control is a key issue throughout the design and development of organizational systems and, indeed, international businesses.

Head office influence

Head office influence is often pronounced in bureaucratic organizations. Many decisions on resource allocation are administered through a tightly knit set of departments and managers, with the head office being the guiding light of the decision-making process. The systems and procedures which control many of the actions taken in bureaucratic organizations tend to be designed by the senior management team based at head office. The influence of head office can lead to a growth in central departments and information systems to extract regular management reports on the activities of the international subsidiaries of the business.

Organizational politics

The bureaucratic organization can foster internal politics, which, if not managed successfully, can lead to disruptive behaviour within the company. Company politics will exist in any organization but can manifest itself quite successfully in an international business where decision-making and resource allocation are concentrated in the hands of a very few managers. The strict demarcation and reporting lines of communication that exist in a bureaucratic business can lead to an intense atmosphere of political disruption which can be detrimental to the business as a whole.

Continuity

As discussed earlier in this section, the advantage of control can be achieved by the bureaucratic organization, and in terms of conducting international business this advantage is often sought by senior managers. Another key advantage sought by bureaucratic organizations is continuity and the perceived benefit achieved by having a stable and clearly defined organizational structure. The career structures can be described to new managers quite easily and an understanding of the company can be achieved through the use of detailed organizational plans and in-depth experience of the workings of the business.

Centralization of activities

The centralization of company activities can have distinct advantages of economies of scale for the bureaucratic organization. The centralization of purchasing departments in particular can have a notable affect on the use of resources within an international business. Another function which can be heavily centralized is production, with major production centres being located close to the key markets to gain specific cost advantages; marketing may also be centralized in the bureaucratic organization and this can lead to standardization of the marketing programmes available to the company and eventually offered to individual markets.

Keeping ideas and expertise

The hoarding of ideas throughout the company may also take place based on the premise that 'knowledge is power', and excluding other departments and functions from access to information can strengthen your position in the hierarchy. This may be true in a bureaucratic organization because of the very hierarchical nature of decision-making within the company.

Inflexibility

Another common aspect of the bureaucratic organization is the inflexibility that can develop as a result of the hierarchy which exists in the company. Inflexibility can also be a result of the extended decision-making process within the company and the nature of communication. The focus on centralization can lead to inflexibility in terms of production facilities, which are difficult to relocate following a change in the needs of the marketplace.

Inflexibility can occur in the management development approaches used by companies and in their affect on strategic planning and strategic thinking within the company.

Teaching

The emphasis in the bureaucratic organization is placed on showing people how to conform to the established procedures and systems used within the company. The established methods of running the company are to be taught to willing and intelligent managers who understand their position in the hierarchy and the effect the development programmes they undertake will have on their career within the company.

NETWORK ORGANIZATION

The network style of organization is not a direct alternative for every international business but perhaps it could be viewed as a target for many international businesses to work towards in the future. You may recognize some of these elements in the international companies you have studied, and increasingly you will see aspects of these approaches being considered or actively introduced into your company. Below are some of the changes that may be pursued by international businesses of the future.

Leaders

The network organization places a strong emphasis on leadership, not only at senior management level but also at team-leader level throughout the company. The term 'leader' has replaced the term 'manager' and has a direct link to levels of self-reliance and responsibility to be found in the company. The need is for people who openly accept the accountability and responsibility that go with leadership and the necessity to be creative in terms of seeking new methods of work and understanding of the demands of existing and potential customers.

Interdependence

The nature of the network-style organization is centred on the growing need for interdependence between different elements of an international business. The lack of resources, or the need to conserve resources, has placed a great deal of pressure on international companies to foster cooperation in terms of business activities. The interdependence is between suppliers and companies at the centre and their end-users. Interdependence is pronounced amongst certain departments who have traditionally found it difficult or non-beneficial to cooperate with each other; for example, manufacturing working closely with marketing planning, human resource management working closely with marketing and purchasing working closely with the supplier network.

Roles and responsibilities

The roles and responsibilities of the network organization change and refocus on the customer and the decision-making process of the company. Roles are varied and support the previous point of interdependence, in that the roles of people within companies are having to overlap and an understanding of a variety of skills is required to outperform the competition.

Horizontal communication

The emphasis in the network organization is on communication at any cost; in fact the organization will not operate successfully unless it has an excellent communication network. The network-style organization is built on effective communication systems throughout the length and breadth of the company. The communication system is often supported by a complex management information system which values information and enables ideas to be transferred quickly throughout the company. The aim of the network organization is not the control of communication and information, but the dispersal of information and access to information for as many people as possible, both internally and externally.

Empowerment

The network organization encourages devolved decision-making and freedom of action throughout the company. This can be interpretated as anarchy or chaos by some international businesses, but the benefits for the organization are increased levels of motivation and confidence amongst people in the company and a faster process of decision-making. Empowerment of people can also lead to greater levels of loyalty towards the company, an increased level of acceptance of responsibility and a tendency to exhibit higher levels of initiative in designing and implementing company programmes.

Effective customer interface

Enhancement of the relationship with the customer is a key aim of the network organization. The empowered and flexible workforce is attempting to meet the needs of each customer in a more specific and userfriendly manner. The pressure to change the organization to meet the needs of the customer is the driving force behind the increased emphasis on the customer interface. Many international companies now believe that the only way to change the fortunes of their company is to develop close and effective customer relationships.

Cooperation

The interdependent nature of the network organization promotes high levels of cooperation amongst the employees throughout the company. The network cannot afford to waste good ideas and duplicate effort in different parts of the world; if an idea is successful in the USA and if the formula is good perhaps it could be tried in the UK with very little adaptation and therefore without additional cost to the company. Close and cooperative internal and external relationships are paramount for the success of the network organization and you can imagine the difficulties and time needed to secure them.

Change

Change is perceived to be the norm of behaviour in these types of organizations, and the people within the company are motivated towards the expectation of change in terms of organizational structure and working environment. The argument for the network organization is often based on its high level of responsiveness to the need and desire for change. This could be a distinct advantage over the bureaucratic organization, which could be viewed as too large to turn around, but the network organization may become too complex and interlinked to reshape.

Delegation

An active policy of delegation is encouraged throughout the company and this is supported by the empowerment strategy of the network organization. The policy of delegation is closely linked to the decision-making process within the company and it enables decisions to be made closer to the customer and promotes development amongst leaders in the company. Delegation is central to the success of the network organization and requires competent leadership throughout every level of the company.

Sharing experience

The sharing of experience is normally an outcome of the network organization and can enhance overall effectiveness of the company. A change in organizational culture is fundamental to the success of the process of sharing experience which takes place in international companies. The network organization has to work towards a value system which reinforces the desire amongst employees to share expertise and knowledge in order to implement company procedures and systems.

Responsiveness and flexibility

Responsiveness is defined in terms of changing the organization to meet the needs of the marketplace and the demands of the customer. Flexibility of response is important because it enables international businesses to meet the needs of their customers in new and different ways. The structure of the company can allow sales people to focus on the needs of individual customers and conduct business development exercises in the search for new business. The delegation of authority which takes place in international networks can provide managers with greater flexibility of decision-making and allow them to make decisions which are more attuned to the needs of local markets and customers.

Learning

The learning organization can support the network organization by providing managers with opportunities to learn and develop new and interesting skills and levels of knowledge. The emphasis is not on teaching, which can be viewed as directive and structured, but on motivating the people within the organization to search for learning opportunities which can deliver a higher level of service and productivity for the customer. Financial resources need to be made available within the network organization so that high levels of interest can be built in the process of continuing education within the organization.

BUILDING INTERNATIONAL ORGANIZATIONS: PRACTICAL GUIDELINES

The building of international organizations with flexible structures and systems for people to use is a difficult task and requires a great deal of effort, thinking and cooperation throughout the company. You will probably have recognized some of the elements just outlined in your own organization and may be considering how your company could introduce some of these initiatives.

Let's consider what is required to build the foundations of a successful international organization.

Encouraging international networking through all communication channels

The communication that takes place between all levels of people in an international business is vitally important in building an international network because it is this interaction which helps to form personal and business relationships within a company environment. The channels of communication have to be fast and efficient and require a high level of investment to ensure their effectiveness. The communication between the operations side of the business, research and development and marketing has to be informal and cooperative for the network style of organization to take root. The sales team need to feel comfortable in speaking to the research and development department concerning a new product or service idea and taking constructive criticism of their business idea or opportunity.

Providing opportunities for informal contacts throughout the company

The new international company implies an organization which is connected by technology and uses technology to communicate ideas throughout the company. The technology exists but there is still a need for a degree of personal and regular contact with colleagues throughout the company. The research and development teams need to understand the problems faced by the sales force when operating in certain markets. The senior strategists of the company require a detailed understanding of the needs of the country managers operating in specific locations. This problem of informal contacts can best be achieved through the use of regular briefing sessions between senior management and regional or country managers with an emphasis on listening to points of view rather than telling managers the new strategy of the company and expecting them to accept the changes without question.

Replacing national procedures with international procedures

The replacement of national procedures and systems with international procedures can enable managers and company personnel to adapt to changing circumstances much more easily. If an international company has an international procedure which is clearly understood throughout the company it can be easier for people to adapt to a changing environment because they will not have to learn a whole new series of systems and procedures. These procedures could include the identification of new business opportunities, the recruitment and selection of people, the assessment procedure for identifying new market opportunities, and operating procedures for new facilities or technology.

Strengthen the functional and business-sector units instead of national units

The functional units can be strengthened instead of the individual businesses in an attempt to build specific functions which cut across the length and breadth of the organization. These functions will be able to take a global perspective on the business and support individual business-sector units throughout the company. An example might be the marketing function of an international company that has a small but well-resourced research and strategy unit at the centre of the company which is able to support individual business units in the struggle to understand the changes taking place in their marketplace. The human resource management function could also be organized in this manner to facilitate the movement of key personnel throughout certain regions more effectively, to organize and implement training and development initiatives, and to design and implement a career structure throughout the company.

Promoting international participation in planning

Encouragement of managers at all levels in the strategic planning process of the company is the aim of the network-style organization. This involvement can take the form of briefing sessions by senior management on the thinking behind the vision statement of the company. These briefing sessions can be organized to listen to the viewpoints of individual managers and to ask them to consider the effect of the vision statement on the activities of individual parts of the business. The strategic planning process has to involve managers throughout the company if it is to be successful because it is the individual managers who adjust the strategic plans of the business to suit the needs of the marketplace.

Building mutual respect for different business cultures

The management development programmes introduced by the international company can assist in promoting the understanding of business cultures by focusing the attention of managers on the difficulties of managing across borders. This will impact on the organizational culture of the company and needs to be carefully managed by the senior management team of the company.

The strategic leadership of the company is paramount in the development of a mutual understanding of cultures across the company; the personalities involved in the senior management team and the manner in which they conduct business will have a profound effect on the search for understanding between the different the business cultures of the organization. This is an area which is often overlooked by organizations as they attempt to take a global perspective on world markets.

Encourage the sharing of resources

The sharing of resources is often forced on the network organization because of the competitive pressures that exist within the company to find quicker and more effective methods of doing business. Resource-sharing does not restrict itself to financial issues; it also includes business concepts and ideas which can be easily transferred throughout the company and utilized to advantage in different parts of the world. It is based on a high level of cooperation being sought and built on throughout the company. This level of cooperation is imperative if resource-sharing is to take place.

Develop integrated international telecommunications

The communication channels used by the company require a tele-communications support system which can enable a fast response from key people within the company. The telecommunications system has to be designed around the needs of the people within the organization and must support the everyday activities of the sales force, purchasing function, marketing, human resource management and operational aspects of the business.

The development of an integrated telecommunications system does not require the latest technology but it does require an understanding of what is available in the telecommunications marketplace for the company to utilize. Adaptation of the technology to the circumstances of the company is important and it is imperative to set up a telecommunications system which can be tailored to your specific communication and working needs.

Move power towards the customer and away from the centre of the company

The concept of moving power towards the customer has been with us since the early 1990s and the network-style structure can allow you to do just that. The focus on the growth of the headquarters of large international companies is in decline and the emphasis is being placed on diffusing power throughout the organization in an effort to achieve higher levels of customer responsiveness and flexibility in operational issues. The aim of some international companies is to identify the individual needs of their customers and to design specific products and services that can meet those needs. The new organizational style would seem to fit the requirements of these needs and may be worth serious consideration by a range of organizations.

It offers advantages over the bureaucratic organization in at least eight key areas of business activities:

1 Sharing company resources and information.
2 Real involvement in strategic planning.
3 Open and informal channels of communication.
4 Customer responsiveness.
5 Managerial motivation.
6 Acceptance of change.
7 Building interdependence throughout the company.
8 Creating a learning environment.

PHILOSOPHY: THE INTERNATIONAL BUSINESS OF THE FUTURE

The international business of the future will certainly need many of the following aspects to be part of its weaponry when it does business and to assist in the development of a dynamic corporate philosophy:

- a clear customer focus which determines and responds to customer needs very effectively;
- increased use of teams to solve organizational problems;
- systems and processes which promote open communication throughout the company;
- continuous review of the organizational activities;
- international networks;
- senior management commitment;
- promotion of leadership;
- competent staff at the centre;
- assigned decision-making responsibility;
- rational and synergistic organizational structures;
- senior management leadership in setting overall company goals.

Exercise 13: Organization and management

Choose two countries or markets to examine in some detail. Brief description:

- Market 1

- Market 2

Once you have chosen the country or market, select from the list below the methods that are used to manage people within those particular markets:

Method	Market 1	Market 2
management development		
career planning		
sophisicated reward systems		
selection tests		
appraisal schemes		
human resource planning		

Method	*Market 1*	*Market 2*
■ employee relations strategy		
■ communications planning		
▓ computerized human resource systems		

Compare the methods used by the company in both markets on a scoring system of 1 to 10 to assess whether they improved the effectiveness of your operations in those markets; if not, why not?

Exercise review:

This exercise should enable you to outline the human resource management systems used by your organization and to compare the effectiveness of those systems in two markets of your choice. The existence of a human resource management strategy will assist the implementation of many of the systems you will outline.

A comprehensive and continuous review of your organizational systems, structure and people is imperative as this aspect of international business is finally being recognized as a serious source of sustainable competitive advantage.

Trends are continually showing that in international business the companies that have converted their innovative strategies into new products have taken market leadership of their chosen sector of operation. Effective management of the abilities of the key people within the company will form a major part of the competitive race of the future. Companies will need to create the correct organizational structure to suit the needs of the individual rather than the company. The focus will be on individual motivation of company workers in an interdependent network-style organization.

One of the key questions facing many international businesses is whether the skills and management philosophies of the successful countries and corporations can be exported into new markets. The characteristics of successful management systems focus on innovation, participative decision-making and an organization based on community and opportunity. Many companies are only starting the journey towards these attributes, and with the advances being made in technology and the concept of networking, the advantages are only starting to be reaped by successful international companies.

6 Global issues for companies

The global issues facing companies will change on a frequent basis and it is difficult for many companies to cope with all of these challenges at the same time. We have clarified what international business is, developed methods of understanding the business environment, designed an overseas market information system, identified the alternative methods of market entry, formulated a sustainable competitive advantage and considered the organizational structure required for the international business of the future.

We have integrated many concepts and you should have used analysis and imagination in many of the examples and exercises in this book. An enduring international business strategy needs to be aware of the global factors that are likely to impinge on the organization in the future. You may have consulted another source to discover the factors which have influenced the thinking and actions of international businesses, and that process can only assist your understanding of the existing and emerging challenges faced by your international business. The views highlighted in this chapter are very much a personal insight.

In this final chapter I have outlined some of the aspects of the business environment and the activities of companies which will have a significant impact on the success or otherwise of international companies in the future. These issues are quite diverse but have clear links in the search for competitive advantage for many organizations.

The first group of factors includes the market opportunities and investment strategy of an international business and will still play an important role in decision-making in many companies.

The second group of factors will be the increased emphasis on the customer and this is likely to continue and will strengthen the focus of many companies towards customers and their individual rather than group needs. This will be supported by a strong emphasis on marketing strategy and the desire for new thinking in terms of marketing strategy and its impact on the customer. The international business of the future will be strongly focused on innovation as a means of securing competitive advantage, and this focus will be not only on new products and services but also on developing a strategy to encourage an innovative culture within the company.

The third group of factors which are of importance will be the extent and success of the business culture of international businesses and the ability of companies to adapt their business cultures to a changing business environment. These will be supported by good management of a diverse range of employees and the implementation of new human resource strategies that enable 'people-power' to become an integral part of international business strategy. The glue that will enable international businesses to build successful business cultures and successful human resource management strategies will be the power, flexibility and lower cost of technology.

The final group of factors includes a drive towards enhancing competitiveness on a continuous basis through business reviews and company transformation. The strategic review of the totality of the business is likely to continue as many companies still search for the ultimate advantage in the methods used to manage their businesses. The search may include the use of partnership power to secure increased levels of intra-company cooperation and efficiencies. Increasingly, as companies attempt to develop business concepts that have a global reach to a set of customers with complex needs, continued pressure will be placed on senior managers to adopt a global strategy to the introduction of new business concepts.

Future competing factors include the following, which are grouped in Figure 6.12.

- emerging markets;
- transfer of service concepts;
- business culture;
- people-power;
- power of technology;
- partnership power;

Figure 6.12 Groups of competing factors

- marketing orientation;
- innovation;
- competitive drive;
- customer focus.

GROUP 1

Emerging markets

The recent emergence of the Bucharest stock exchange caused barely a ripple on the global marketplace. Neither did the announcement of the plans of the Indonesian financial community to have its own stock exchange in the near future. Emerging markets are always more interesting and exciting to the potential investor than the mature markets of the USA, Japan or Europe. The choice for potential investors may focus on global emerging markets, investment trusts or geographical or regional investment areas. Chile is very similar to Singapore in the way it is developing and expanding as an economy. Since the mid-1980s, as emerging markets have put in place tougher market regulations on one level and imposed stricter fiscal measures to combat high inflation on a higher economic plane, individual markets have attracted huge inward investment flows.

Between 1960 and 1980 the Brazilian and South Korean markets more or less marched in step, with steady or even high levels of annual growth of up to 10 per cent. Following this period their paths diverged dramatically, with the Korean economy maintaining steady growth, while Brazil attempted to interfere in the market economy and high and dramatic inflation resulted. Countries of interest for the investor could be economies which are closely linked to the American dollar, such as Malaysia or Thailand, but interest seems to be moving towards economies with tenuous dollar ties, such as India, Korea and Taiwan. In Latin America, favoured markets are Brazil, Peru and Columbia, with Mexico and Argentina currently neutral. The emerging markets could also be in Eastern Europe and, in particular, in Poland, Romania, Hungary and the Czech Republic.

These are some of the aspects you could explore within your company:

- economic changes in the global markets;
- investment horizons;
- opportunities to invest in new markets;
- developing new markets;
- portfolio of investments.

GROUP 2

Customer focus

A strong customer focus can develop a customer-driven organization which views the customer as 'king' in an increasingly competitive and customer-biased business environment. The lead can be taken by service-based companies making customer care a paramount factor to consider in the future strategies of international business. The emphasis on customer care as a fundamental component of competitive advantage will increasingly be realized by service-based companies as they struggle to achieve an increased level of market share.

Expenditure on customer-friendly procedures and systems are to be viewed as an investment in the future success of the company. The experiment of home shopping currently being explored by a series of companies will expand quite dramatically in the future. The link between technology and customer focus will be recognized and companies that take advantage of this link will be in a good position to exploit the customer-friendly environment of the future.

Some of the aspects you could explore within your company are:

- the global customer;
- how to develop new markets;
- how to establish a typical customer profile;
- how to match product and service quality;
- quality plus creativity – how to add more than just quality.

Case outline: American Express

The emergence of a series of global brands in the financial sector has been quite dramatic, and with the advances taking place in technology this trend can only gather pace. The fundamental challenge faced by many of these leading financial companies is to balance the local demands of markets whilst maintaining a global vision for the company and a system of innovation and product development to support the international vision of the company.

How can you coordinate the organizational pressures to meet the needs of local customers by using detailed technology to analyse the ever-changing desires of the international customer? Central coordination across borders and the local operations of individual subsidiaries are placing increased demands on the skills of the senior management teams within these companies.

The intangibility of many services places an additional pressure on companies to establish workable systems of brand management to propel the company past the competition. American Express is an international company which has managed to develop extensive international coverage which actually provides a barrier to entry for new competitors and is necessary to support the marketing claims made by the organization. National responsiveness is now being recognized as a key method of leveraging competitive advantage is these rapidly developing markets.

The development of services is at the forefront of many of the initiatives being explored by international companies and it requires a responsiveness to customer needs which has not previously existed. American Express is one example of a company managing to adapt to the changing needs of a technically aware customer.

Marketing orientation

International companies must develop products and services which are needed and desired by customers and which are ahead of the competition's offerings. The definition of the customer has to be very clear and the organization must be structured to deliver high levels of customer satisfaction. This means having a lean organizational structure and efficient and effective service supported by a decentralized marketing staff; and developing all company staff with a set of marketing skills which are linked very closely to a formal set of marketing plans and strategies.

Knowledge of the market trends needs to be widely available throughout the company, and the analytical skills of segmentation, targeting and positioning must be understood and used within the management and marketing teams of each international business. The systems needed to support the marketing expertise of the company will have to include analysis of customer intelligence, competitor intelligence reports and product-line profitability analysis. These will be supported by marketing, planning and control systems which give your international business confidence in the future and a strong competitive advantage. Rewards and recognition systems should support the marketing initiatives being taken in the company and promoting individual effort throughout the business.

Emphasis can be placed on the individual customer by means of formalized vision and mission statements which lead marketing actions in the company. The strategic marketing plan of the international business has to have precise marketing objectives and a strong commitment from senior management towards implementation. You could explore the following aspects within your company:

- world-class marketing;
- named customers;
- customer loyalty;
- relationship-based marketing;
- customer as 'partner';
- 'one-to-one' communications.

Case outline: McDonalds Corporation

The business world is changing rapidly even for the mainstay of the American fast-food industry. The need to interpret the desires of a diverse customer base continues to be a challenge for the company. The McDonalds Corporation has recognized that individual customers have replaced products and the marketplace as the key drivers of the global village and of the products those customers expect.

The desire to focus the marketing effort of the company very clearly on the perceived and implied wants of the customer is at the heart of the marketing strategy of the company. The company will need to innovate around its established product range and even offer services which have not yet even been considered.

Levels of customer satisfaction will need to be measured in a more sophisticated manner and this will involve the use of technology and an advanced range of customer feedback systems. The pressure is on companies such as McDonalds to place the customer at the centre of their international business strategy and deliver higher levels of customer satisfaction. One method of achieving this focus on the customer is to keep the mission statement firmly fixed on the customer and to train employees to deliver ever higher levels of customer service. This may warrant a new drive towards active collaboration between the·customer and the company.

Innovation

Innovation and creativity are the keys to competitive advantage: establishing an on-going programme of innovation in the expansive and technologically intensive international markets that many companies are now operating within; recognizing that the product strategies of your company must be supported by a strong corporate culture. You need informed and committed people to handle the current and increasingly complex innovation process in an effective and cost-focused manner. Today, corporate culture is coming into focus as a tool for gaining competitive advantage. Increases in research and development spending are an important factor in ensuring success in innovation, even though research and development may be focused in many centres throughout the world and across a series of continents.

Making the most of an innovative culture is based on a deliberate and rigorous commitment to technological development within an organizational culture which is focused on customer needs and which encourages personal creativity.

Idea-generation using technology can be an important way forward for many international companies. Companies as diverse as banks and oil companies can generate business ideas and challenge standard practices by linking technology and networks to enhance the creative process. Ideas can be channelled to a central position within the company, where they can be evaluated and screened before investment is considered. The process can be assisted greatly by utilization of the views of external advisers, who may not have any direct contact with your business but can view the idea independently and comment objectively.

These are some of the aspects you could explore within your company:

- innovative strategies;
- creative teams;
- innovation-based business cultures;
- innovation as a competitive weapon;
- innovative people.

GROUP 3

Business culture

The business culture of many international companies has stressed empowerment strategies and this has given them an edge in the marketplace, or so they believe. Encouraging the correct business culture in some organizations is achieved through the active promotion of responsibility, loyalty and individual initiative. These international companies believe that only people with self-esteem and a feeling of power can take responsibility. They experience and create a clear meaning within a company by achieving goals which they have agreed and for which they have consciously taken real responsibility. People who choose not to take responsibility in organizations may find it very difficult to create meaning in their organizational life. Their behaviour will tend to be controlled by rewards and sanctions from others; they will only see a point in making what they feel is an extra effort if they can gain an advantage or disadvantage.

Some international companies are developing a business culture which can enable people to assume responsibility. Each person assumes responsibility and understands and acts upon a set of clearly agreed roles and personal/organizational objectives. This requires less focus on the role and importance of the manager, a change in the attitude of many business managers towards people, a change of attitude among many of the employees, and a move away from the traditional methods of allocating assignments and responsibilities which exist within many international business units. Senior management plays a key role in ensuring that responsibility is diffused throughout the company. This requires a high degree of courage on behalf of senior managers, the promotion and building of self-esteem within the company and the ability to accept the competence of individuals and to instill confidence in other people regarding their own capabilities.

Some of the aspects you might like to explore within your own company are:

- the role of top management;
- how companies will find top people;
- international working practices;
- flexibility in the workforce;
- empowerment vs freedom;
- motivation through the business culture.

People-power

An awareness of the changing needs of the customer and the overall business environment is required to ensure that the initiatives being taken are appropriate and allow the international business to build a successful partnership between its people and the appropriate customer groups. This will be particularly important when international businesses are seeking to take advantage of the service industries of tomorrow. The maxim of being close to the customer has to be monitored effectively to test whether the 'people-initiatives' being tried by the organization are indeed delivering enhanced customer and service benefits.

The international business that learns to trust its employees will benefit from a fast reaction to changing customer needs and implementation of new ideas. The UK oil company British Petroleum has introduced a computerized network of communications between various parts of the world to enable the successful transfer of ideas that have been tested or introduced in other parts of the business. This system encourages communication throughout the company, as well as the non-duplication of ideas and faster implementation of new concepts throughout the world.

Investment in any international business is governed by a range of business needs and pressures, and the aim of people-power in many international businesses will be to create a high level of creative activity within the company which can help it compete in the marketplace. The requirement in many international businesses will be to recognize the importance of the creative process and, once investment is agreed, to ensure that investment is consistently available to enhance the creative response of the company. The range of organizational structures required is complex and their design must be clearly based on the needs and motivations of key customer groups.

Below are some aspects for you to consider within your company:

- the number of people that will be required in the future;
- international competencies;
- changes in employment patterns;
- composition and ability of the workforce;
- development as an incentive;
- rewarding the international manager of the future.

Power of technology

The virtual organization driven by technology is now a reality for many international companies and the search is on for competitive advantage through the power of technology. We are in the middle of the ITT revolution: information, telephones, technology. This is a revolution that will fundamentally change the way international businesses work, communicate and do business. The use of technology needs to be harnessed because of the incredibly cheap and powerful software available to companies, inexpensive and powerful personal computers and the introduction of portable computers. These developments are supported by new digital telephone networks using ISDN and creating an instantaneous set of connections and access to computer networks providing vast bandwidth, as much as 128 Kbps for the cost of two telephone calls, at nearly the speed of a local-area network clogged with traffic.

The new technology environment is based on electronic documentation, with local-area networks everywhere and supported by well-developed electronic mailing systems. Many of these advances in technology are coordinated by a hub system, which may take the form of technical support for a sales team, technical systems to move information around the international business, or office space for the hub workers and visiting company employees. Documentation products and systems will be used as standard by many companies, and the use of groupware products will continue to increase dramatically in many industries and sectors of international business.

Within your company you could consider the following:

- the virtual organizations;
- local response through technology;
- future technology needs;
- new developments;
- technology in search of an application;
- hardware or software.

GROUP 4

Competitive drive

The competitive drive will be led by the large organization and the professional manager; this was certainly the strong view of commentators in the late 1960s and may still be true in some areas of business. Many large American corporations are restructuring and dramatically changing management systems and increasing the focus on customer responsiveness and quality. New approaches to strategic management are being introduced to complement these changes. The new approaches are designed to stimulate innovation and customer awareness and contribute to the cultural changes that need to accompany restructuring when it is being introduced.

New ideas centre on redefining the business mission and visions of international companies to make them more relevant to the changing needs of the marketplace. Companies are integrating the central activities of the business in an attempt to stimulate more entrepreneurial activity and business development opportunities. There is an increased focus on customers and their changing needs, financial performance measures and improved levels of quality throughout the company. Changing the behaviour of managers and employees who have made their international careers within the previous command and control structure is difficult and challenging for many businesses. However, such behavioural change is essential if international businesses are to achieve the innovation, the competitiveness and the surges in productivity that are often sought in the drive towards competitiveness. These are some of the aspects to explore:

■ competitive benchmarking;
■ regenerating core strategies;
■ developing a distinctive and far-sighted competitive strategy;
■ taking the lead over competitors;
■ constant transformation;
■ beyond restructuring.

Partnership power

The impact of increased global competition and technological change has driven many international companies to take a fresh look at the totality of their business and the international markets in which they operate. They have had to make a strategic analysis of the whole complex set of relationships involved in bringing a finished product or service to the final customer. The complexity of these relationships will obviously vary quite considerably between one company and another. A shortened term for this set of supplier–customer relationships is the supply chain. In practice most goods and services reach the customer through a mix of different supply chain relationships.

For many international businesses, innovative supply chain developments are still at an early stage, and many of the benefits are still quite fragmented and variable. The ways in which companies are collaborating include: sharing information; integrating systems; collaborative training strategies; shared project teams in customer companies and across the supplier network. There is a need to meet the challenge of foreign competition in speed of innovation and production and in quality and price, following the example set by the Japanese ways of working collaboratively with networks of small suppliers. This is facilitated by new information systems and automated manufacturing processes. A continually renewed awareness of the market and the need to meet customer requirements is a fundamental element of developing effective partnerships throughout the supply chain.

You might like to explore these aspects within your company:

■ starting partnerships;
■ using partnerships to enter new markets;

- success or failure in strategic partnerships;
- the challenge of making the partnership work;
- business partnerships between stakeholders.

Transfer of service concepts

The transfer of a service concept is a difficult proposition for any company and should be approached with the utmost care and attention. Many new markets will not have any experience of the service, which may have been successful in quite a different market. Often success can be achieved only by a high level of investment in advertising or a particularly unique service which has an established reputation and mass appeal. International businesses will be able to develop a new range of services based on technology and customer convenience, but at the moment many international businesses will be looking to established services to find international opportunities. For example, in the United States the services that will be easily recognizable by the customer will centre on business, professional and technical services. Other services that could be attractive to the US customer may focus on education, financial services, insurance, telecommunications, computer and data processing and legal services.

It is unlikely that UK businesses operating from a UK base can offer effective and competitive operations for non-specialized services that are easily provided by US-based competitors. There are, however, a number of areas where British businesses can be successful in selling services, and these include:

- European export marketing services;
- establishment of strategic alliances;
- mergers and acquisitions;
- setting up European satellite offices;
- warehousing and distribution services;
- sourcing products;
- advice on legislative requirements, standards and economic data;
- specialist advice on quality assurance;
- training services.

These may prove to be a starting point for the ideas bank of many international businesses.

Below are some of the aspects you could explore:

- developing the global business concept;
- adaptability of the business idea;
- generating concepts;
- introducing concepts into new business environments;
- success and failure.

Exercise 14: Future global issues

Why not consider the ten key factors that you believe will have an impact on your company or a company you have been researching?

- Factor 1:

- Factor 2:

- Factor 3:

- Factor 4:

- Factor 5:

- Factor 6:

- Factor 7:

- Factor 8:

- Factor 9:

- Factor 10:

Exercise review:

You may find that the factors you have identified are quite different from the ten that I have discussed in the rest of the chapter. It may be interesting to compare the factors you have identified and explore some of the issues surrounding these points with your colleagues in the company.

Perhaps you could set up a communication network throughout your company to highlight and discuss the key factors facing the future of your company in the late 1990s and beyond. A starting point could be a strategy workshop or management development programme specifically designed to force the key issues out into the open for detailed discussion to take place. These initial steps could form the basis of an action plan to address the competing factors facing your company and the management initiatives needed to move confidently into the future.

An opening agenda for these initial steps could be based on the following questions:

- How creative is your future investment strategy?
- Does your company culture adapt to the changing business environment?
- How focused are you on the needs of individual customers?
- Do you understand the competitive nature of your business?

If you examine these questions in small groups of five or six interested colleagues and endeavour to explore the issues in some detail you may be surprised at the answers and the success of the process.

TOWARDS THE NEW MILLENIUM

One point is very clear. The future is unlikely to be as straightforward as the past, and many of the successful international managers are aware of that fact. If the stalwarts of the 1980s, such as IBM, are struggling to compete, with all their management and forecasting skills, what chance does a mere manager have of surviving in the turbulent final years of this century and indeed the first few years of the next?

What we are witnessing is a change in the major players in the international game of business and an increasing reliance on three elements: people, technology and innovation. The challenge for many international managers is to master these changes. In attempting to increase their skill levels in technology, manage effectively across borders and translate new ideas into action, the same challenges will face international companies as face international managers.

This book will support the actions you take in building a successful international business. Your initial understanding of the business environment must be complemented by a detailed analysis of the changing nature of the international marketplace and the behaviour of the customer. The market entry strategy should be competitive and be managed effectively on a strategic and operational level at all times. This means that the future will be challenging and exciting, and this book will assist you in understanding some of these challenges and starting the process of continually meeting the needs of the global marketplace.

— *Notes*

PREFACE

1 Further guidance for those who wish to develop international business strategy can be found by contacting (in writing) Neil Coade, Coade Management Consultants Limited, c/o International Thomson Publishing, Berkshire House, 168–173 High Holborn, London WC1V 7AA.

INTRODUCTION

1 For further insight into the required skills and factors for international success, contact Neil Coade (see note 1).
2 *Ten Reasons to Talk to 3M* etc., Public Relations Department, 3M UK PLC, 3M House, PO Box 1, Bracknell, Berkshire RG12 1JU.
3 Corporate Affairs Department, Nissan UK.

1 UNDERSTANDING THE BUSINESS ENVIRONMENT

1 *Trading With China, A Practical Guide to Doing Business in China*, Department of Enterprise, London, United Kingdom.

2 MARKET ANALYSIS

1 See case study/articles on leading international companies from Japan, such as Komatsu.

3 DEFINING THE MARKET ENTRY STRATEGY

1 See information provided by the British Overseas Trade Board and the Department of Enterprise, both based in London, United Kingdom.

4 DEVELOPING A SUSTAINABLE COMPETITIVE ADVANTAGE

1 Dave Francis (1994) *Step-By-Step Competitive Strategy*, Routledge.
2 The author acknowledges the influence of Michael Porter and, especially, the key frameworks contained in *Competitive Advantage*, Free Press, 1985.

5 ORGANIZATION AND MANAGEMENT

1 Colin Coulson-Thomas (1992) *Creating the Global Company*, McGraw-Hill.

— *Further reading*

There are many books and articles which are relevant to those seeking to develop their skills in managing international business. These are my recommendations.

Bradley, F. (1991) *International Marketing Strategy*, Prentice Hall.
Coulson-Thomas, C. (1992) *Creating the Global Company*, McGraw-Hill.
Deal, T.E. and Kennedy, A.A. (1982) *Corporate Cultures*, Addison Wesley.
Francis, D. (1994) *Step-By-Step Competitive Strategy*, Routledge.
Garrison, T. and Rees, D. (1994) *Managing People Across Europe*, Butterworth & Heinemann.
Ohmae, K. (1991) *The Borderless World*, Fontana.
Peters, T.J. and Waterman, R.H. (1982) *In Search of Excellence*, HarperCollins.
Phillips, C., Doole, I. and Lowe, R. (1994) *International Marketing Strategy*, Routledge.
Porter, M.E. (1992) *The Competitive Advantage of Nations*, Macmillan.
Porter, M.E. (1985) *Competitive Advantage*, Free Press.
Segal-Horn, S. (1994) *The Challenge of International Business*, Kogan Page.
Schein, E.H. (1985) *Organizational Culture and Leadership*, Jossey Bass.
Stonham, P. (1994) 'Change in the Global Economy: An Interview with Rosabeth Moss Kanter', *European Management Journal*, vol. 12, no. 1.
Usunier, J.-C. (1993) *International Marketing*, Prentice Hall.
Yip, G.S. (1992) *Total Global Strategy*, Prentice Hall.
Young, S., Hamill, J., Wheeler, C. and Davies, J.R. (1989) *International Market Entry & Development*, Harvester Wheatsheaf.